Here We Stand

COMMEMORATING THE 500TH ANNIVERSARY OF THE REFORMATION

REFORMED
FREE PUBLISHING
ASSOCIATION
Jenison, Michigan

© 2018 Reformed Free Publishing Association

Unless noted the scriptures cited are taken from the King James (Authorized) Version

Reformed Free Publishing Association
1894 Georgetown Center Drive
Jenison, Michigan 49428
rfpa.org
mail@rfpa.org
616-457-5970

Cover design by Jeff Steenholdt
Interior design and typesetting by Katherine Lloyd/the DESK online.com

ISBN 978-1-944555-37-5 (hardcover)
ISBN 978-1-944555-38-2 (ebook)
LCCN 2018937059

Contents

IMPORTANT CITIES OF THE REFORMATION

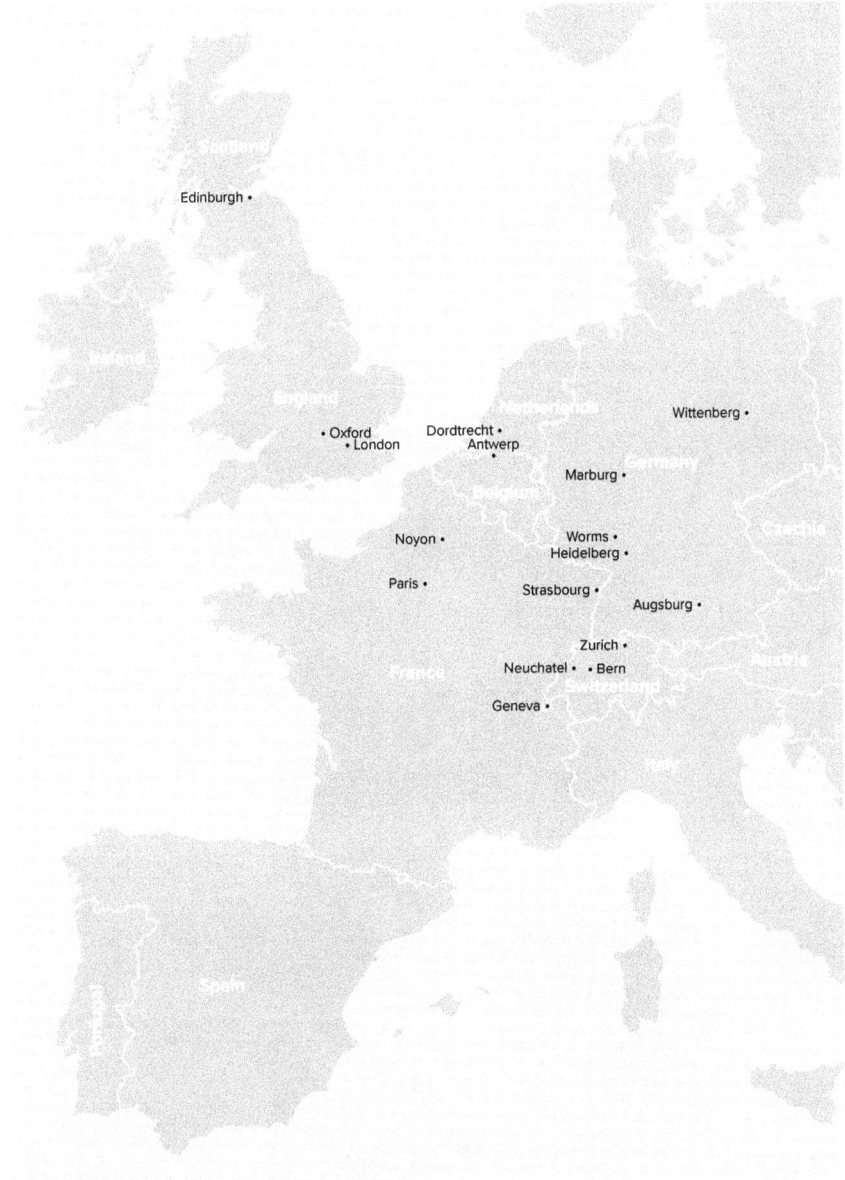

Edinburgh •

• Oxford   Dordtrecht •   Wittenberg •
   • London   Antwerp

Marburg •

Noyon •   Worms •
            Heidelberg •

Paris •   Strasbourg •
             Augsburg •

Zurich •
Neuchatel •   • Bern

Geneva •

Editor's Preface

This is a little book that commemorates the anniversary of a great event. That great event was the Reformation of the church in the sixteenth century. The one church at that time, the Roman Catholic Church, had become thoroughly corrupt and had fallen away from the truth of the word of God. Over the centuries, it had become grotesquely deformed. Through the work of Martin Luther, John Calvin, Ulrich Zwingli, John Knox, and others, the church was reformed. Purity of doctrine and holiness of life were restored to the church.

Because these men reformed the church, they are remembered collectively as the reformers. They were men of conviction, not ambition. They were men with servants' hearts, not self-seeking. They were men who were interested in serving Jesus Christ, not promoting self in the place of Christ. They were men who sought the glory of God, not the praise of men.

And God used them—mightily! He used them in different places and through diverse circumstances, but all of them in very much the same way. He used them in their preaching and teaching—and they were all great preachers. He used them in their writings—they were also prolific writers. He used them not only to reprove the church for her errors and false worship, but he used them to restore to the church the truth of the gospel and the right worship of God. Through the reformers, the church was brought back again—back to Augustine, back to the early church, back to the apostles, and most importantly, back to the word of God.

In October 2017, the church commemorated the five hundredth anniversary of the great Reformation, if we mark, as is usually done, Luther's nailing of the Ninety-five Theses to the door of the church in Wittenberg on October 31, 1517, as the beginning of the Reformation. That act of Luther, under the providence of God, set in motion a series of events, all of which culminated in the Reformation. The Reformation changed the entire landscape of Europe, even from a political, social, and economic point of view. Nevertheless, the Reformation was not essentially a political, social, or economic movement. It was a religious event that aimed at changing conditions in the church. And it did—in many different ways, under the providence of God. It did! The church was never again the same. In the providence of God and under the blessing of God, the Protestant and Reformed churches were birthed.

To commemorate the five hundredth anniversary of the Reformation, the Protestant Reformed Theological Seminary organized a conference. The conference was spread over two days and included six hour-long speeches. The theme of the conference was: "Here We Stand!" That theme, of course, was taken from Martin Luther's famous words before the Diet of Worms: "Here I stand!" The conference was very well attended, and the speeches were well received. It was not merely a joyful celebration of an event that took place in the past. It was also a grateful acknowledgment of a treasure and tradition that had been graciously bestowed. And it was, hopefully, a way in which to endear to the up-and-coming generation the precious heritage that is ours as heirs of the Reformation.

Already before the conference took place, the Reformed Free Publishing Association (RFPA) approached the seminary and expressed an interest in publishing the speeches in book form.

We readily agreed, anticipating that the value of the conference would thereby be greatly enhanced. You hold in your hand the finished product. I wish to express thanks to the RFPA for considering the worth of publishing the speeches. Also I wish to express thanks to all the speakers, not only for giving their speeches, but for doing all the additional work of expanding and transcribing their speeches as chapters in this book.

Please do not suppose that the chapters in the book are merely transcripts of the speeches that were given at the conference. Much work has been done to enhance each of the speeches by adding material that could not be included in the conference speeches because of time constraints. It is our hope that our readers will find the book to be of value, whether they learn some things that are new or are reminded of things they had forgotten—all of them vital truths of the great Reformation. Then, after you have read the book, recommend it to others as a valuable refresher course on some of the most important aspects of the Reformation. Now read and enjoy!

Ronald Cammenga, editor
Wyoming, Michigan
January 2018

Chapter 1

WHAT WAS THE REFORMATION? A STRUGGLE TO ENJOY THE ASSURANCE OF SALVATION

Ronald L. Cammenga

≈

*Therefore being justified by faith, we have peace with God
through our Lord Jesus Christ.*
—ROMANS 5:1

This book celebrates the Reformation—the great Reformation of the church in the sixteenth century. What was the Reformation? In simplest terms, the Reformation was the doctrinal and spiritual renewal of the church in the sixteenth century.

The one, great church of that day was the Roman Catholic Church. Over time the church had become thoroughly corrupt and apostate. Errors of doctrine and wickedness of life characterized both clergy (officebearers) and laity (church members). From top to bottom the church was filled with unbelief and immorality. The church taught and the people believed the errors of works-righteousness, free will, the papacy, the priesthood, purgatory, the authority of tradition above the authority of the word of God, and many other false doctrines. In his last letter to Pope

Leo X, in the preface of his treatise on "The Freedom of a Christian," Martin Luther wrote:

> The Roman church, once the holiest of all, has become the most licentious den of thieves [Matt. 21:13], the most shameless of all brothels, the kingdom of sin, death, and hell. It is so bad that even Antichrist himself, if he should come, could think of nothing to add to its wickedness.[1]

In a work entitled "The Babylonian Captivity of the Church," Luther lamented:

> How wretchedly and desperately all the activities of the church have been confused, hindered, ensnared and subjected to danger through the pestilent, ignorant, and wicked ordinances of men, so that there is no hope of betterment unless we abolish at one stroke all the laws of men, and having restored the gospel of liberty we follow it in judging and regulating all things.[2]

The great work of the Reformation was a work accomplished by God. It was not the work of man. Great men though they were, Luther, Calvin, Zwingli, Knox, and the others did not bring about the Reformation. They were merely the instruments by which the Reformation took place. Several years after the Reformation had begun, Luther looked back and is reported to have said, "Like a blind mule I was led by Christ." The reformers regarded the Reformation as God's work through his Spirit. The Reformation was

---

1 Martin Luther, "The Freedom of a Christian," in *Career of the Reformer I*, in *Luther's Works*, ed. Jaroslav Pelikan and Helmut T. Lehmann, American edition, 55 vols. (Philadelphia, PA: Muehlenberg and Fortress, and St. Louis, MO: Concordia, 1955–86), 31:336.

2 Martin Luther, "The Babylonian Captivity of the Church, 1520," in *Word and Sacrament*, in ibid., 36:102–3.

the fulfillment of the promise that Christ made to his disciples in John 16:13 that he would give them the Spirit, the Spirit of truth, who would lead the church into all the truth. The Reformation stands in the history of the New Testament as the proof of Jesus' promise to his disciples in Matthew 16:18 that not even the gates of hell would prevail against his church in the world.

One of the most important aspects of the Reformation was that it restored to the people of God the assurance of their salvation. Assurance—this was the very issue that sparked the Reformation. The Reformation began over Martin Luther's personal struggle for the assurance of his salvation. Luther was brought up in a dark religious climate of doubt and fear. The church of his day denied the very possibility of assurance even to the most faithful. No matter how diligently one made use of the means of grace, attended mass, followed the traditions of the church, and lived in obedience to the dictates of the pope, he could not have the assurance of his salvation.

Luther himself experienced a great personal struggle to come to peace with God and the assurance of his salvation. It was only after he came to understand the truth of justification by faith alone, apart from man's own work, that he also came to the assurance of his salvation. When he no longer depended on his own works but on the perfect work of Christ, and not on his own merits but on the eternal merit of Christ, then the way was opened for Luther to enjoy the assurance of the Christian life.

Luther's struggle is the struggle of every child of God, in every age. It is the struggle of the child of God who knows himself, as Luther knew himself, to be a lost, unworthy sinner. It is the struggle to possess the assurance, the undoubted assurance, of one's own personal salvation in the light of the conviction concerning our sinfulness. It is the struggle to possess the assurance that God is your God, your loving heavenly Father. It is the struggle to enjoy the assurance of election, one's own personal election, that you are one of God's elect children. It is the struggle for the assurance that God's Son, Jesus Christ, has died for you, even for you. It is the struggle to know that you are indwelt by the Holy Spirit, the Spirit of regeneration and faith. It is the struggle to enjoy the assurance that the Spirit who applies all the blessings of salvation will also preserve you in your salvation.

It is the struggle for the assurance that you are and forever shall remain a living member of Christ's church, as the Heidelberg Catechism expresses it in Lord's Day 21.[3] It is the struggle for the assurance that nothing is able to separate you from the love of God in Christ Jesus the Lord, as the apostle Paul says in Romans 8:35. It is the struggle to know that everlasting life and glory await you after the trials and sorrows of this life—the crown of righteousness that Paul confidently expected according to 2 Timothy 4:8. It is the struggle to possess the assurance that dispels every fear: fear of God's wrath, fear of hell, fear that things in this life might be against you. How blessed is the person who possesses this assurance! How miserable, utterly miserable is the person who does not enjoy this assurance!

AN EXPERIENCE IN LUTHER'S OWN SOUL

God used Luther's own personal struggles to prepare him to reform the church. Apart from his own personal experiences, Luther never could have been the reformer that he became. As God used Moses' experiences in the deserts of Midian to prepare him to be the deliverer of his people, and as God used David's

---

3 Heidelberg Catechism A 54, in Philip Schaff, ed., *The Creeds of Christendom with a History and Critical Notes*, 6th ed., 3 vols. (New York: Harper and Row, 1931; repr., Grand Rapids, MI: Baker Books, 2007), 3:325.

years of tending his father's sheep to prepare him to be the king of Israel, so God used Luther's own personal experiences to fit him to be the mighty reformer of the church.

Already early in his life, Luther experienced unrest over the assurance of his salvation. His struggles only intensified as he grew older. Especially troubling to him was the prospect of death, and after death facing a just and holy God.

Men and women living in sixteenth-century Europe were much more familiar with death than we are today. For them death was a persistent reality and an ever-present threat, whether by disease, war, or famine. There was widespread poverty, which inevitably took its toll on human life. Unsanitary conditions were the norm, contributing to the rise and rapid spread of many diseases. What today are very treatable diseases were death sentences in sixteenth-century Europe. People who were healthy one day might be dead and buried the next day. Childbirth was an especially risky proposition, for both the baby and the mother. Once born, many children never reached adolescence. More than one-third of all the children born in the sixteenth century died before their sixth birthday. Life expectancy was under forty years of age. Mercilessly death stalked the men, women, and children who lived in the century of the Protestant Reformation.

In the spring of 1505, while Luther was studying at the University of Erfurt, an epidemic of the Black Plague swept through the city. Also called the Black Death or the Bubonic Plague, historians estimate that this gruesome and painful disease killed some fifty million people. Today the disease is effectively treated with antibiotics. But in the sixteenth century there were no antibiotics. In approximately one hundred years, nearly half of Europe's population succumbed to the dread disease. It was spread by infected fleas that infested the rats that were abundant in the cities of this era. With a great deal of open garbage and raw sewage, the rat population in the cities swelled, and right along with it the fleas carrying the bacteria that caused the Bubonic Plague.

Symptoms of the disease included black-colored boils all over the infected person's body, chills, high fever, vomiting, muscle cramps, seizures, swollen lymph nodes, extreme pain in the infected areas, gangrene of the extremities (toes, fingers, lips, and nose), difficulty breathing, coughing, delirium, coma, and finally death. So widespread was the plague's devastation that nearly everyone lost an immediate family member, and in some cases whole families and villages were wiped out.[4]

Shortly before this new outbreak of the plague, Luther had received the stunning news that his brothers Heintz and Viet had died of the disease. Now the town of Erfurt and its university were infected. Death was everywhere throughout the city. Black crosses that marked infected homes hung on door after door. The carts carrying the dead to the cemetery rumbled through the streets at all hours of the day and night. Because of the great number of victims, the stench of death and decay was everywhere in the city.

The university was hit especially hard. Many faculty members and scores of students died of the plague, a number of whom Luther knew personally. Classrooms were half-empty and many classes were cancelled because the professor who was teaching the class died. One of Luther's closest friends succumbed just before they were to receive their master's degrees. That was an especially severe blow for Luther, and he struggled to understand the wisdom of God's ways.

All of this set Luther to thinking: "What if it's me? What if I

---

4   Herman Selderhuis, *Martin Luther: A Spiritual Biography* (Wheaton, IL: Crossway, 2017), 41–42.

am the one infected with the plague? What if I die? Will I be able to stand before God? Will I be righteous before him, or will he banish me from his presence forever?"

"I WILL BECOME A MONK"

Because he was beset by doubts and fears concerning his own salvation, Luther left the study of law in order to become a monk. The ascetic, self-denying life of the monastery offered Luther the possibility of peace and assurance. The questions in Luther's soul were: "How can I, a sinner, be righteous before God? How can I have the assurance that God is my God and Jesus Christ is my savior?" The Roman Catholic Church answered those questions by saying that a man must work. Assurance of salvation must be earned or merited. By what a man did, at least in part, he earned his standing before God and the assurance of his salvation.

At the time that Luther entered the monastery, he believed the teaching of the church. For this reason he became a monk. Becoming a monk or nun was viewed as an especially good work. As a monk, Luther endeavored with all his might to obtain the assurance of his salvation by his own works. He prayed and fasted. He engaged in various acts of self-denial, even beating himself. Willingly he performed the humblest of tasks around the monastery. He ate very little food, until he nearly wasted away and looked like a walking skeleton. In his room, which was called a cell, even in the middle of the winter he had no heat and slept on a mat on the floor with no covers. About his life as a monk, Luther later said:

> I was a good monk, and I kept the rule of my order so strictly that I may say that if ever a monk got to heaven by his monkery it was I. All my brothers in the monastery

will bear me out. If I had kept on any longer, I should have killed myself with vigils, prayers, readings, and other works.[5]

But in the way of trying to earn his salvation, Luther could not come to the assurance of his salvation. He had no peace in his soul, no inner confidence, no certainty that he was a child of God. Work as he might, he stood in constant terror of the wrath of a holy God. Luther once said, "Though I lived as a monk without reproach, I felt that I was a sinner before God with an extremely disturbed conscience. I could not believe that he was placated by my satisfaction."[6] In his recently published biography of Luther, Eric Metaxas correctly assesses this phase of Luther's life:

> In 1507, Luther was a monk and an ordained priest. But it wasn't enough simply to be a monk. Now he had to do what monks did: be scrupulous in his prayers and his thoughts and constantly confess the slightest unscrupulousness that he could see in these areas. Whereas it would be wrong to suggest other monks didn't take all of this seriously, one gets the impression that Martin Luther took it about as seriously as anyone ever could, and because of this he bumped hard into the limitations of this life in a way that few ever did, which in turn is precisely what caused him to think about the whole religious system in a way that few ever did.[7]

---

5   Quoted in Roland Bainton, *Here I Stand: A Life of Martin Luther* (New York, NY: Abingdon-Cokesbury, 1950), 45.

6   Martin Luther, *Career of the Reformer IV*, in *Luther's Works*, 34:336.

7   Eric Metaxas, *Martin Luther: The Man Who Rediscovered God and Changed the World* (New York, NY: Viking, 2017), 42.

THE MERITS OF OTHERS

If Luther could not arrive at the assurance of his salvation through his own works, perhaps he could rely on the works and merits of others. This, in fact, was also the teaching of the Roman Catholic Church of Luther's day, as it is the teaching of Rome still today. Rome taught that many of the saints, especially the blessed virgin Mary, had done many more good works than were necessary for their own salvation. Their "leftover" good works were called works of supererogation. The merit of those works constituted a great treasury, which could be transferred to those whose accounts were behind, that is, to those who lacked sufficient merits of their own to earn salvation. This transfer was done by the church through the pope or the pope's representatives. Such a transfer of merit was called an indulgence.

Indulgences, of course, were purchased. The sale of indulgences was a huge money-making scheme that the medieval Roman Catholic Church had invented. It brought a great deal of revenue from all over Europe into the coffers of the pope. Besides obtaining indulgences for oneself, it was possible to secure an indulgence for a relative or friend who had died and was suffering the pains of purgatory.

The church connected the dispensing of the merits of the saints with visitation of their relics. Again, this was something for which visitors paid. The greatest storehouse of relics was in the city of Rome, the seat of the popes and the nerve center of the Roman Catholic Church. It was alleged that in Rome there were the remains of forty popes and more than 76,000 martyrs. Rome was supposed to have a piece of Moses' burning bush and links from the chain with which the apostle Paul had been bound, as well as some of the bones of Peter and Paul. In Rome one could view the pieces of money that had been paid to Judas Iscariot in order to betray Jesus; whoever viewed these coins obtained an indulgence of 1,400 hundred years from the sufferings of purgatory. In Rome was the white marble staircase with its twenty-eight steps that supposedly stood in front of the palace of Pontius Pilate, the very stairs which Jesus had climbed on Good Friday. The staircase was known as the *Scala Sancta*. Helena, the mother of the emperor Constantine the Great, had the staircase brought from Jerusalem to Rome. No city on earth was so plentifully endowed with holy relics and with indulgences as Rome.

For this reason, Luther was overjoyed at the opportunity to visit Rome in 1510 in order to conduct some official business on behalf of his monastic order. During the month that he was in Rome, Luther sought to take full advantage of the spiritual benefits that the city afforded. Besides performing the daily tasks assigned to him in the Augustinian cloister in which he lodged, he visited and celebrated mass at numerous sacred shrines, visited the catacombs and the basilicas, and venerated the bones and sacred relics of countless saints.

But in the end, Luther's doubts persisted. For one thing, he was stupefied by the ignorance, pleasure madness, and immorality of the Roman clergy. He was also horrified by their irreverence for that which was holy and their apparent unconcern for spiritual things. After he returned from Rome, Luther is reported to have expressed agreement with the adage, "If there is a hell, Rome is built over it."[8] What shattered Luther's confidence and fueled the doubts with which he was struggling were the supposed merits of the saints and the merits attached to visiting their sacred shrines. More and more he came to see these for what they were: crass money-making schemes intended to take advantage of the poor

---

8   Thomas M. Lindsay, *Luther and the German Reformation* (Edinburgh: T. and T. Clark, 1900), 44.

and the ignorant. Luther climbed Pilate's staircase on his hands and knees, repeating the Lord's prayer on each step, and kissing each step for good measure. Later he said that when he reached the top he said to himself, "Who knows whether it is so?"[9]

Not in his own works, nor relying on the works and merits of others, could Luther possess the assurance of his salvation. "Peace, peace," the church said. But for Luther there was no peace.

RECOVERING THE GOSPEL OF GRACE

By his own bitter experience and through God's providential leading, Luther was brought to see that the only possibility for assurance of salvation is through faith in Jesus Christ. The gospel of grace is the possibility of assurance—the only possibility. Apart from it, there can be no enjoyment of the assurance of salvation. In Christ alone, *solus Christus*, through faith alone, *soli fide*, by grace alone, *sola gratia*, is the possibility of salvation and the assurance of salvation.

Because the Reformation was a recovery of the gospel of grace, it was also a recovery of the assurance of salvation. It was a recovery of the truth of assurance—the only basis and ground of assurance. And it was the recovery of the actual experience and enjoyment of assurance by believers.

The possibility of assurance is by faith, Luther came to see. The possibility of assurance is true faith that looks away from self and looks instead to Jesus Christ. Assurance is enjoyed through a faith that trusts not in our own works or in any other works of man, but that trusts alone in the perfect work of Jesus Christ. That is the faith that brings the believer assurance. This is the only ground for assurance! Apart from faith in Jesus Christ there is no assurance, no enjoyment of peace in heart or mind. Apart from faith

9 Bainton, *Here I Stand*, 51.

in Jesus Christ there is only doubt and fear, anxiety and despair. Apart from faith in Jesus Christ there is only the sense of God as an angry and righteous judge before whom every man must one day stand and to whom we must all eventually give account.

One of the most troubling aspects of the Reformation to the Roman Catholic authorities in Luther's day was that at long last believers began to know whom they believed and to be assured of their salvation. It was the wonderful Reformation truth of justification by faith alone that was the key to open the door of assurance. When Luther understood that his standing before God did not depend on himself, on his own works or merits, on who he was or what he did, but depended instead on Jesus Christ alone, the fears and doubts that for so long had troubled him were dispelled as mist before the rising sun. When Luther understood that his righteousness before God was not due to his works but was due to the finished and perfect work of Christ, he experienced what he never had experienced in the way of working to earn his salvation: peace with God. It was the peace that the apostle Paul speaks of in Romans 5:1: "Therefore being justified by faith, we have peace with God through our Lord Jesus Christ." It was the peace that the prophet Isaiah spoke of long ago in Isaiah 32:17: "And the work of righteousness shall be peace; and the effect of righteousness quietness and assurance forever." At last, peace, perfect peace!

In his *Table Talk*, Luther is reported to have said:

> Nothing is more sure than this: he that does not take hold on Christ by faith, and comfort himself herein, that Christ is made a curse for him, remains under the curse. The more we labour by works to obtain grace, the less we know how to take hold on Christ; for when he is not known and comprehended by faith, there is not to be expected either

assurance, help, or comfort, though we torment ourselves to death.[10]

Note what Luther says: when Christ "is not known and comprehended by faith," we cannot expect "comfort, though we torment ourselves to death." Luther had nearly tormented himself to death, but despite all those torments, he did not enjoy comfort. Trusting in Christ, he found what he could not find trusting in himself.

GOD'S WILL THAT HIS PEOPLE ENJOY ASSURANCE

An important aspect of Luther's recovery of the truth of assurance was that Luther came to see that it is God's will that his people live and die in the assurance of their salvation. The Roman Catholic Church of Luther's day and the Roman Catholic Church of today not only deny the possibility of the assurance of salvation, but deny that assurance is the will of God for his people. That is the stranglehold that the Roman Catholic Church has on its members. The only possibility of assurance of salvation is living in obedience to the church. But even the most faithful can never attain the unfailing assurance of their salvation. The best for which they can hope is years spent in the agonies of purgatory until finally they are delivered from the fires of purgatory into the glory of heaven.

The Roman Catholic Council of Trent was convened in 1546 in order to stem the tide of the Reformation. In one of its many decisions taken in opposition to what the reformers were teaching, the council denied the possibility of the assurance of salvation in this life.

---

10 Martin Luther, *The Table Talk of Martin Luther*, ed. Thomas S. Kepler, trans. William Hazlitt (Grand Rapids, MI: Baker Books, repr. 1995), 114.

No one, moreover, so long as he is in this mortal life, ought so far to presume as regards the secret mystery of divine predestination, as to determine for certain that he is assuredly in the number of the predestinate; as if it were true, that he that is justified, either cannot sin any more, or, if he do sin, that he ought to promise himself an assured repentance; for except by special revelation, it cannot be known whom God hath chosen unto himself.[11]

It is not the will of God that his people generally possess assurance. Only the select few to whom God gives a special revelation may have the assurance of their salvation.[12]

There are those, even in the Reformed tradition, who have viewed the Christian life as a life of perpetual doubt and fear. There have been those who lived and died in what seems to be a proud lack of assurance of salvation. They at least are not like so many professing Christians who take their salvation for granted. Oh, no! It must be given, this assurance of salvation. If you have not been given this assurance, you are not to be blamed, and there is nothing that you can do but wait for it to be given. Others have contended that assurance must be sought, and that only after rigorous efforts, throughout most of one's lifetime, is it finally attained. There have been ministers in this tradition who aimed in their preaching to create doubt among the members of the

---

11 Canons and Decree of the Council of Trent, sixth session, "On the Gift of Perseverance," in Schaff, *Creeds of Christendom*, 2:103.

12 Interestingly enough, the Arminians at the time of the Synod of Dordt also took the position that only they who receive a special revelation from God may have the assurance of their final salvation and preservation in salvation. For this reason, article 10 of the fifth head of the Canons of Dordt begins as it does: "This assurance, however, is not produced by any peculiar revelation." Confer Schaff, *Creeds of Christendom*, 3:594.

church, rather than to comfort repentant sinners with the good news of the gospel.

It must be admitted that in our superficial and hypocritical age, when many profess to be Christians but live very much like the world, it is tempting to go in this direction. In our day, there are many who are at ease in Zion, content with outward membership in the church, as were many of the Jews in Jesus' day. These people prided themselves in the fact that they had Abraham to their father and that they had been circumcised in the flesh. Today many rest their confidence in the fact that they were born into Christian families, were baptized and brought up in the church, were educated in the Christian schools, and have made an outward profession of faith. But we must not correct one error by introducing another equally pernicious error. The normal Christian life is not a life lived in doubt and fear; neither is it a life lived in false confidence. But the normal Christian life is a life lived in the assurance of faith, that is, in the assurance of salvation through faith in Jesus Christ.

Luther understood from scripture that it is the will of God not only to save his people, but also to give those whom it is his will to save the assurance of their salvation. He saw from God's word that it is God's will to give believers the assurance of salvation in this life, here and now. He contended that this is the normal experience of the Christian.

That is a wonderful thing, indeed! It would be wonder enough if it were only God's will to save us, but never to give us the assurance of our salvation in this life. That would be grace, indeed, because no one deserves salvation. It would be grace if in the end God saved us and took us to heaven to live with him, but all our life long he never gave us the assurance of salvation, so that we could never be certain that we were saved. Then we would live all of our life in doubt and fear, not knowing for sure whether or not we were the objects of God's grace, although in the end we would be brought to heaven and given the enjoyment of heaven's bliss in the presence of God and Jesus Christ. But God's salvation is even more wonderful and his grace even more amazing. For it is God's will not only to save us, but to give us already in this life the assurance of our salvation.

It is God's will to give us the assurance that he is our God, our loving heavenly Father who is for us and never against us. It is his will to give us the assurance that Christ died for us, even for us, and made satisfaction to God for the guilt of my sin, even mine. It is his will to give me the assurance that the Holy Spirit dwells in me, has regenerated me, and has given to me the gift of faith so that I believe in Jesus Christ and walk thankfully in all good works.

Luther insisted that the assurance of salvation was the normal experience of the Christian—part of salvation itself.

> But when the heart has doubts…it is also driven in a short moment to blasphemy and despair. For this reason St. Paul so often urges us to have full assurance…that is, a firm and unshakeable knowledge of God's will toward us, which gives assurance to our consciences and fortifies them against all uncertainty and mistrust. The teaching of the pope is all the more detestable because it not only disregards this but even wickedly maintains that one should have doubts; that is, he publicly declares God a liar, even though he promises, swears, pledges His majesty, and curses Himself.[13]

---

13 Martin Luther, *Lectures on Genesis Chapters 21–25*, in *Luther's Works*, 4:144–45.

Commenting on David's familiar words in Psalm 23:1, "The LORD is my shepherd," Luther wrote:

> For faith is and must be a confidence of the heart which does not waver, reel, tremble, fidget, or doubt but remains constant and is sure of itself. A similar idea is expressed in Is. 40:8: "The word of our God will stand forever." It "stands," that is, it is steadfast, it is certain, it does not give way, it does not quiver, it does not sink, it does not fall, it does not leave you in the lurch. And where this Word enters the heart in true faith, it fashions the heart like unto itself, it makes it firm, certain, and assured. It becomes buoyed up, rigid, and adamant over against all temptations, devil, death, and whatever its name may be, that it defiantly and haughtily despises and mocks everything that inclines toward doubt, despair, anger, and wrath; for it knows that God's Word cannot lie to it.[14]

In his lectures on the sermon on the mount, Luther often treated the matter of the assurance of salvation. In his comments on Matthew 5:8: "Blessed are the pure in heart: for they shall see God," he said:

> It is a wonderful thing, a treasure beyond every thought or wish, to know that you are standing and living in the right relation to God. In this way not only can your heart take comfort and pride in the assurance of His grace, but you can know that your outward conduct and behavior is pleasing to Him…All the monks have publicly taught that no one can know whether or not he is in a state of grace. It

---

14 Martin Luther, *Notes on Ecclesiastes, Lectures on the Song of Solomon, Treatise on the Last Words of David*, in ibid., 15:272.

serves them right that because they despise faith and true godly works and seek their own purity, they must never see God or know how they stand in relation to Him.[15]

In his sermons on the gospel of John, preaching on John 15:4: "Abide in me, and I in you. As the branch cannot bear fruit of itself, except it abide in the vine; no more can ye, except ye abide in me," Luther railed against the "doctrine of the pope" and "all factions" who nullify faith and the assurance of salvation through faith in Jesus Christ. They "say about pious people, who are upright and perform good works" that they "are not to know how they stand with God." Luther went on to say that "the vile and accursed devil from hell told them to say and proclaim this!"[16] A bit later, Luther expressed the judgment "that it is intolerable to declare in Christendom that we cannot and must not know whether God is gracious to us." He went on to counsel every "Christian pastor or a believing Christian" that he must profess and say, "I know that I have a gracious God and that my life is pleasing to him."[17]

That it is the will of God that believers enjoy the assurance of their salvation, the scriptures make abundantly plain. For one thing, scripture proclaims the blessed truth that God is our heavenly Father. What Christian parents would be satisfied only to provide for their children, giving them plenty of food, adequate shelter, and sufficient clothing? What Christian parents would be pleased only that their children feared and obeyed them? What Christian father or mother would be satisfied with that? Do not Christian parents want above all else that their children know that they love them, love them more than anything in the entire world? Do not Christian parents do everything that they can to reassure

---

15 Martin Luther, *Sermon on the Mount and the Magnificat*, in ibid., 21:38.
16 Martin Luther, *Sermons on the Gospel of St. John Chapters 14–16*, in ibid., 24:217.
17 Ibid., 24:221.

their children of their love for them, surrounding them with the tokens of their love, so that their children have that assurance? How much more is this not true of God, our heavenly Father, in relation to those who are his children?

Scripture also teaches that God is the husband of the church. The church is his bride and wife. What Christian husband would be satisfied only with providing for and protecting his wife? What Christian husband would be content that his wife honor him, submit to him, and cook and clean for him? Is it not rather the case that a Christian husband desires more than anything else that his wife loves him and knows of his love for her? Does he not repeatedly remind her of his love and constantly surround her with the tokens of his love? We need to do more of that than we do as Christian husbands. If everything is right in a Christian marriage, the husband not only loves his wife, but constantly reassures his wife of his love for her.

That is what Christ, the head and husband of the church, does. He does that in his word, his love letter to his beloved bride. That is what holy scripture is and the purpose that holy scripture serves. In its pages Christ proclaims his everlasting love for his bride, the church. In the preaching of the gospel, Christ assures his church of his love. That is the "good news" that the gospel proclaims: God's love in Jesus Christ for his elect people. Every Lord's day, through the preaching of the gospel, we are confirmed in God's love for us in Jesus Christ. This is one reason—not the only reason, but one reason—on account of which the pure preaching of the gospel and faithful church attendance ought to be of great importance in the life of every Christian.

Many specific passages of scripture make plain that it is the will of God that his people live and die in the assurance of their salvation. Many give expression to the comfort in life and in death that God's people actually enjoy. Think of the book of Psalms and how frequently the psalmists give expression to the assurance of their salvation. To be sure, the psalmists had their struggles with various doubts and fears, as is the case with every child of God. There were the doubts and fears that were due to their own sins and falls into sin. There were doubts and fears that arose in their souls because of the distressing circumstances of their earthly lives. But in the end, they enjoyed the assurance of the love and favor of God.

Think of Psalm 23. In the very first verse, David confesses, "The LORD is my shepherd; I shall not want." That is the assurance of the child of God. He is assured that his Savior is his shepherd, the one who guides him and protects him as he walks down all the different pathways of life. Exactly because he has the confidence that the Lord is his shepherd, he is able to say, "I shall not want." That clearly is the idea of Psalm 23:1. Because the Lord is his shepherd, therefore he is assured that he shall not want. To such an extent is he assured that he shall not want that even "though I walk through the valley of the shadow of death, I will fear no evil: for thou art with me; thy rod and thy staff they comfort me" (v. 4). In the confidence that the Lord is his shepherd, he is even able to face death—death, mind you— with confidence and without fear. The conclusion of the psalm is that "surely goodness and mercy shall follow me all the days of my life: and I will dwell in the house of the LORD for ever" (v. 6).

Or think of Psalm 73. Though for a time the psalmist was envious of the wicked and felt that God was against him, he came to see the truth of the matter: "Truly God is good to Israel, even to such as are of a clean heart" (v. 1). That was the conviction God worked in the psalmist through the hard circumstances of life which he had led him. So the psalmist was brought by God to the assurance, which is the conclusion of the psalm, "Nevertheless I am continually with thee: thou hast holden me by my right hand. Thou shalt guide me with thy counsel, and afterward receive me to glory" (vv. 23–24). Glorious assurance!

Or call to mind the Old Testament patriarch Job. After the Lord had grievously afflicted him, he expressed his doubts and fears, as in Job 19:9–11: "He hath stripped me of my glory, and taken the crown from my head. He hath destroyed me on every side, and I am gone: and mine hope hath he removed like a tree. He hath also kindled his wrath against me, and he counteth me unto him as one of his enemies." Yet he did not lose the assurance of his salvation altogether. Think of what Job confidently confessed just a little later in verses 23–26:

23. Oh that my words were now written! oh that they were printed in a book!
24. That they were graven with an iron pen and lead in the rock for ever!
25. For I know that my redeemer liveth, and that he shall stand at the latter day upon the earth:
26. And though after my skin worms destroy this body, yet in my flesh shall I see God.

What a glorious confession! What an expression of the assurance of salvation enjoyed by the believer!

Over and over again the New Testament teaches the same assurance of salvation that God's elect people enjoy.

15. For ye have not received the spirit of bondage again to fear; but ye have received the Spirit of adoption, whereby we cry, Abba, Father.
16. The Spirit itself beareth witness with our spirit, that we are the children of God:

17. And if children, then heirs; heirs of God, and joint-heirs with Christ; if so be that we suffer with him, that we may be also glorified together. (Rom. 8:15–17)

Think of Paul's glorious confession in 2 Timothy 1:12: "For the which cause I also suffer these things: nevertheless I am not ashamed: for I know whom I have believed, and am persuaded that he is able to keep that which I have committed unto him against that day." "I know whom I have believed," says the apostle and every child of God through the apostle. That is the language of confidence—unwavering confidence.

In the first epistle of John, an epistle that is all about assurance, the apostle John uses similar language. He speaks there of knowing that we know God. In 1 John 3:1–2, the apostle exclaims:

1. Behold, what manner of love the Father hath bestowed upon us, that we should be called the sons [children] of God: therefore the world knoweth us not, because it knew him not.
2. Beloved, now are we the sons of God, and it doth not yet appear what we shall be: but we know that, when he shall appear, we shall be like him; for we shall see him as he is.

That is the assurance of the Christian: that he is God's child and that God has set his love upon him. That gives us confidence for the present and good hope for the future.

In the end, the whole Christian life is built on the assurance of salvation. That underscores the importance of assurance in the life of the believer. There is not and there cannot be a Christian life apart from the assurance of salvation. Why does the Christian do good works? Why does he strive to live in harmony with the will of God? Why do we carry out the demands of our earthly calling, sometimes at great cost? Why do we sacrifice, expend ourselves, endure persecution, and are willing even to lay down our lives for the sake of the gospel? In order to earn or merit with God? No! A thousand times, no! Why? In order to show our love for and our thankfulness to the God who has saved us. That is the reason—the only reason. Our thankfulness to him arises out of and proceeds from our assurance of salvation. How can I be thankful to God for that of which I am not assured? That is impossible. I cannot be. No one can be. True thankfulness presupposes the assurance of salvation. The whole Christian life of gratitude rests squarely on the assurance of our salvation.

"THESE DOUBTS AND FEARS THAT TROUBLE ME"

This is not to deny that there are times when doubts and fears arise in the soul of the child of God, even the strongest of God's children. There are times in the life of every Christian when he succumbs temporarily to these doubts and fears. We sing in Psalter 210 concerning "these doubts and fears that troubled me."[18] In Psalm 77, of which Psalter 210 is a versification, the psalmist speaks of crying out to God in "the day of my trouble" (v. 2). He complains that his "spirit was overwhelmed" and that he was "so troubled that [he] cannot speak" (vv. 3–4).

Even after Martin Luther's recovery of the gospel of grace and the assurance of salvation that he enjoyed through faith in Jesus Christ, there were times when he struggled with various doubts and fears. There were times, in fact, when he struggled mightily

---

18 No. 210:5, in *The Psalter with Doctrinal Standards, Liturgy, Church Order, and added Chorale Section*, reprinted and revised edition of the 1912 United Presbyterian *Psalter* (Grand Rapids, MI: Wm. B. Eerdmans Publishing Co., 1927; rev. ed. 1995).

with these doubts and fears and was even incapacitated by them temporarily. That is the experience of every child of God. No Christian escapes such struggles. Some experience these struggles to a great extent than others, to be sure, but no one escapes these struggles altogether.

There are especially two sets of circumstances in the Christian's life that often result in his being plagued with doubts and fears concerning his salvation. This may, first of all, be the result of sin and impenitence in sin. When the Christian walks in sin, when he stubbornly refuses to repent of his sins, when perhaps he is living secretly in sin, God in his just judgment takes away from him the assurance of his salvation. The Canons of Dordt speak of this in head 5, where the fathers of Dordt affirm that in the way of impenitence, the children of God may very well "interrupt the exercise of faith, very grievously wound their consciences, and sometimes lose the sense of God's favor for a time, until, on their returning into the right way of serious repentance, the light of God's fatherly countenance again shines upon them."[19]

The sight and sense of our sins can also cause us to doubt our salvation. That was David's experience, as he relates it in Psalm 51. The background of this psalm is the sins of David in committing adultery with Bathsheba and murdering Uriah. The history of this "lamentable fall" of David, to use the language of the Canons of Dordt, is recorded in the book of 2 Samuel, chapters 11 and 12.[20] For some time, David went on impenitent in these sins. During that time, he did not "hear joy and gladness" and felt as those his bones had been broken (v. 8). His experience was that of someone who had been cast away from God's presence (v. 11). During this time, he lost "the joy of [his] salvation" (v. 12).

---

19 Canons of Dordt 5.5., in Schaff, *Creeds of Christendom*, 3:593.
20 Canons of Dordt 5.4, in ibid.

In Psalm 32, which has the same historical background as Psalm 51, David says that during the time that he walked impenitently in his sins, "my bones waxed old through my roaring all the day long" (v. 3). He goes on to say that it was his experience that "day and night thy [God's] hand was heavy upon me: my moisture is turned into the drought of summer" (v. 4). That was David's utterly miserable experience, until God brought his sinful servant to repentance. Then, in the way of repentance, God restored to David the assurance of his salvation: "I acknowledged my sin unto thee, and mine iniquity have I not hid. I said, I will confess my transgressions unto the LORD; and thou forgavest the iniquity of my sin" (v. 5).

Every child of God knows the truth of this by his own bitter experience. We have all experienced, as the result of our sins and our refusal to break with our sins, the loss of the assurance of our salvation. God simply will not allow his children who go on in sin against him to enjoy the assurance of their salvation. It is not the case merely that they lose the assurance of their salvation. The reality is that God takes that assurance away from them. That belongs to God's chastening of his people on account of their sins. This is one of the things—this loss of the assurance of their salvation—that God uses to bring his people to repentance. That was the case with David, and that is still God's way today.

But doubts and fears may, in the second place, also be the result of hard circumstances in the life of the child of God. That too is often the case. God may send troubles and trials, grievous afflictions and dread diseases upon us or upon our loved ones. It may be cancer. It may be a debilitating disease. It may be the death of a child or of a spouse. Or it may be the waywardness of a rebellious child or abandonment by an unfaithful spouse. Or a thousand other painful earthly circumstances.

That was the case with Job. He lost everything, absolutely

everything that was dear to him. He lost all his riches, camels, sheep, and oxen, as well as his servants and even his own dear children. Then his wife and his friends turned against him.

In Martin Luther's case, it was the death of his thirteen-year-old daughter, Magdalena. What the devil could not do, what his enemies could not accomplish, the death of his dear daughter nearly did. It brought Luther to the brink of despair. For weeks he was overwhelmed with grief, grief that incapacitated him for his work in God's church. The cause of the Reformation itself was in jeopardy, from a human point of view. But then God used Luther's dear wife, Katie, and his friends, especially Philip Melanchthon, to deliver Luther and restore him again to his family and to his work on behalf of the Reformation.

These sorts of trials in the life of the Christian can shake his faith and cause him to doubt that the Lord loves him. The child of God asks, "How can these things be happening to me, if God loves me and his blessing rests upon me?" An old Puritan once said that it is hard to believe in a withdrawing God, and indeed, it is.

When we are beset by these doubts and fears, it is important that we respond to them in the right way. First, we must remind ourselves and remind one another that it is the will of God that we live in the assurance of our salvation. Trials and tribulations are not necessarily the expression of God's wrath and judgment. They are not sent by God to crush us and to destroy us. In fact, trials and tribulations are not at all inconsistent with God's love for us, as the writer of the epistle to the Hebrews reminds us: "For whom the Lord loveth he chasteneth, and scourgeth every son whom he receiveth" (Heb. 12:6).

Second, the Christian must take a harsh view of the doubts and fears that arise in his soul. He must not minimize them; he must not excuse them. But he must condemn them. Doubt is unbelief, and unbelief is sin! In Romans 14:23, the apostle says, "He that doubteth is damned." When we doubt, we are like Peter, who took his eyes off Christ; and as soon as he did, he began to sink (Matt. 14:28–31).

Third, what is true of every other sin in the life of the believer is also true of doubt. Although he falls into this sin, he does not go on in it indefinitely and impenitently. The dominion of sin is broken in him; he no longer lives in sin, even though sin lives in him. By God's grace and through the Holy Spirit, he is delivered from the power of this sin also. God gives him the victory over this sin and restores to him the assurance of his salvation.

Fourth, the life of the believer is not a life of doubt and fear because he fights against the doubts and fears that do arise in his soul. He does not make his peace with these doubts; he does not feed these doubts; he does not suppose that it is right and normal for him to doubt his salvation; and he certainly does not justify and excuse his doubts. But because he knows that doubt is sin, he repents of his doubts and he fights against his doubts. He prays earnestly to God for the grace of the Holy Spirit to overcome his doubts. God answers those prayers, and God gives his grace and Spirit so that the believer has the victory over this sin in his life. In this way, God preserves the child of God in the assurance of his salvation.

RESTING IN THE CROSS AND WORK OF CHRIST

What must be stressed is that the assurance of the child of God is not at all in his own works or worth. The Reformation was the recovery of the gospel of grace, the grace of God in Jesus Christ, and for that reason it was also the recovery of the assurance of salvation. The confidence of the child of God must not be in his own work, but alone in the finished and perfect work of Christ. The confidence of the child of God must not be in his own worth, but in the worth of the sinless Son of God. By her doctrine of works-righteousness and merit, the Roman Catholic Church robbed God's people of the assurance of their salvation. Luther saw that and knew the truth of it by his own experience.

In his lectures on Genesis, Luther contended:

> For the promise does not depend on my merits or works; it depends on the Seed of Abraham. By Him I am blessed when I apprehend Him in faith; and the blessing clings to me in turn and permeates my entire body and soul, so that even the body itself is made alive and saved through the same Seed.
>
> And that begins in this life through faith when the soul, weighed down by death and sin, is buoyed up and receives the comfort of life and salvation.[21]

Not our works, but faith in Christ gives us standing before God now and in the day of judgment. Luther says that "anyone who takes hold of the Word of God and who remains in faith can take his stand before God and look at Him as his gracious Father. He does not have to be afraid that He is standing behind him with a club, and he is sure that He is looking at him and smiling graciously, together with all the angels and saints in heaven."[22] In another place, commenting on John 14:6 and our Lord's statement, "I am the way, the truth, and the life," Luther says that "[a] Christian is to be sure of his destiny. And since he has Christ, he has everything and would have the right to jump for joy at all

---

21 Luther, *Lectures on Genesis*, in *Luther's Works*, 4:158.
22 Luther, *Sermon on the Mount*, in ibid., 21:39.

times. But all this is according to the spirit and faith in Christ, the Way on which he has begun to travel."[23]

Luther knew that the enjoyment of assurance is only through faith in Jesus Christ. He knew that reliance upon his own works or the works of others could never lead to the assurance of salvation. He knew that there are solid, biblical reasons on account of which our good works can never be the ground of our assurance of salvation.

First, our good works can never be the ground of our assurance because it is impossible for the creature ever to merit with the Creator. God made man perfect and in his own divine image. As the Belgic Confession says, he created man "good, righteous, and holy, capable in all things to will agreeably to the will of God."[24] By virtue of his perfect creation, man was obliged to serve God perfectly. That was his calling. What room was there for any merit, any doing of that which was above and beyond the call of duty? Even in the state of perfection, man could not have merited with God. It is always true, as Jesus says in Luke 17:10, that "when ye shall have done all those things which are commanded you, say, We are unprofitable servants: we have done that which was our duty to do."

Second, besides the impossibility of man's meriting with God, the fact is that our best works are vile, tainted with sin. Our best works—the worship of God, the reading of the scriptures, and our living together in our marriages and families, as well as in the congregation with fellow believers in the communion of the saints—are imperfect and polluted by sin. That is the teaching of the Heidelberg Catechism: "whereas even our best works in this

---

23 Martin Luther, *Sermons on the Gospel of St. John*, in ibid., 24:45.
24 Belgic Confession 14, in Schaff, *Creeds of Christendom*, 3:398.

life are all imperfect and defiled with sin."[25] The prophet says in Isaiah 64:6, "But we are all as an unclean thing, and all our righteousnesses are as filthy rags." For this reason, those who depend on their own good works for their standing before God can never come to the assurance of their salvation. They can never be sure that they have done enough, and they can never be sure that what they have done is good enough. That was Luther's experience as he sought by his works—the works enjoined by the church of his day—to obtain the assurance of his salvation. In the end, seeking assurance in this way can only lead to doubt and despair.

Third, our good works can never be the ground for our assurance of salvation because the good works that the child of God does perform are the good works that God has ordained that he should walk in them. True enough, God accounts them to be our good works. He even rewards the believer for the good works that he does. Right along with that, he forgives for the sake of Jesus Christ the sinful aspects of our good works, so that those good works are purified and are indeed good works. But in the end, they are not our good works, the doing of which we can claim as the ground of merit with God. Rather they are the works that he has ordained and that by his grace he works in us. That is the teaching of the apostle in Ephesians 2:10: "For we are his workmanship, created in Christ Jesus unto good works, which God hath before ordained that we should walk in them." The prophet expresses this same truth in Isaiah 26:12: "LORD, thou wilt ordain peace for us: for thou also hast wrought all our works in us."

But most of all, our good works cannot merit with God and cannot be the ground of the assurance of our salvation because those who trust in their good works for salvation, show contempt

25 Heidelberg Catechism A 62, in Schaff, *Creeds of Christendom*, 3:327.

for the cross of Christ. That is the seriousness of trust in our own works, rather than the perfect and finished work of Jesus Christ. It is disdain for the work that Christ has accomplished by his life of perfect obedience and by his atoning death. There is one work that has standing with God and has satisfied the claims of his justice. That is the work of Jesus Christ. All who trust in their own works, and to the degree to which they trust in their own works, despise the work of Christ. It is to "despise...the riches of his [God's] goodness" (Rom. 2:4) in the cross of Christ. There is no sin greater than contempt for Christ and the work he has done.

For all these reasons, there can be no assurance of salvation so long as we trust in our own works. No work of man can ever satisfy the claims of God's perfect justice. God must satisfy the claims of his own justice. God has done that in his Son, our Lord Jesus Christ. That is the gospel and the good news that the gospel proclaims.

But perhaps the doubts persist: "Am I a saved child of God? Am I really a believer? Do I have faith? Are my sins forgiven? Am I going to heaven?"

I ask you: Do you trust for your righteousness and salvation upon the Son of God, Jesus Christ, alone? Do you depend upon his work, and not at all upon your own works? Is your only confidence in him and in his cross? Do you look for holiness and obedience not to yourself and your own strength, but to him by his grace and Spirit alone? Do your sins trouble you? Are you sorry for them? Do you confess them and fight against them? Do you want to go to heaven, not just because every sorrow, pain, sickness, and death will be gone, but because at last you will be able to see and to serve God without sin?

Then be assured that you are a believer. You need have no

doubt about that, not even for a moment. Regardless of the strength or weakness of your faith, regardless of the need that you have for growth in faith, you have faith. You need not wonder about that or be uncertain regarding it. You are not mistaken or deceived. Rather than to doubt your faith, you must thank God for your faith, and you must diligently exercise yourself for the development and growth of that faith. Like the man who brought his demon-possessed son to Jesus in Mark 9:24, the Christian's cry is, "Lord, I believe; help thou mine unbelief." That is the cry of faith. It takes faith, even great faith, to recognize the weakness of faith. "Lord, I believe;" but then immediately, "Help thou mine unbelief." Faith sees the imperfection of faith. And faith, true faith, cries out to God for the strengthening of faith.

The Lord hears that cry! He always hears that cry! The promise of the word of God is that he will not break the bruised reed or quench the smoking flax. It is the promise that the work of grace that he has begun in us, he will preserve to the very end.

This is God's gift to us in the Reformation—the gift of the assurance of our salvation. The Reformation was not only instrumental in restoring the truth of the gospel of grace, but for that very reason it was also the means of God to restore to the church the assurance of salvation. The result of that assurance is peace and comfort. It is the comfort that is expressed in the first answer of the Heidelberg Catechism:

> That I, with body and soul, both in life and in death, am
> not my own, but belong to my faithful Savior Jesus Christ,
> who with his precious blood has fully satisfied for all my
> sins, and redeemed me from all the power of the devil;
> and so preserves me that without the will of my Father
> in heaven not a hair can fall from my head; yea, that all

things must work together for my salvation. Wherefore, by his Holy Spirit, he also assures me of eternal life, and makes me heartily willing and ready henceforth to live unto him.[26]

He "assures me of eternal life" and through that assurance "makes me heartily willing and ready...to live unto him" in gratitude for his "so great salvation" (Heb. 2:3).

---

26 Heidelberg Catechism A 1, in Schaff, *Creeds of Christendom*, 3:307–8.

Chapter 2

THE REFORMATION'S RETURN TO *SOLA SCRIPTURA*

David Torlach

≋

> *To the law and to the testimony: if they speak not according to*
> *this word, it is because there is no light in them.*
> —ISAIAH 8:20

The prophet Isaiah spoke these words when Israel—the visible church of that day—had departed a very long way from the truth. Israel was seeking knowledge, wisdom, guidance, and life from everything around them. They were seeking these things from the heathen idols, from the philosophies of the pagan religions, and even from the created, physical earth. But they had ceased to seek after God and after his revealed word.

It is God's revealed word, the holy scripture, that is meant by "the law" and "the testimony." If a "law" or a "testimony" exists, then it only exists because it has been brought into existence and developed by someone. The "someone" in this text is Jehovah God: Isaiah is referring to God's law (the Hebrew is "Torah," referring to the first five books of the Old Testament). A "testimony" is a witness or attestation of truth, and Isaiah is referring to the other scriptures, to God's witness concerning himself and his truth in his written word. As this is God's truth, we may say that this is *the* law and *the* testimony, before which all others pale into insignificance.

Isaiah is telling us (that is, the church of that day, together with all churches in every age and place) that we have a perfect witness and a perfect law. It belongs to, and is given by, God, who is the creator and upholder of the universe. God has given that word perfectly, moving holy men by the Holy Spirit, so that what they spoke and wrote was not the words of men, but rather the infallible counsel of God (2 Tim. 3:16–17; 2 Pet. 1:20–21). The Lord has not left himself without a witness (Acts 14:17). That witness is the infallible scripture, which we hold in our hands. Therefore, Isaiah says, scripture *is* the standard by which everything (note: *everything*) is judged. The Holy Spirit reveals to us that if anything is held up to the pure light and truth of the Bible and does not harmonize with it, it is because that thing, that teaching, that practice, lacks light and truth.

This wonderful and central doctrine, proclaimed by Isaiah, is repeated in various ways throughout the Bible, and this is the essence of *sola scriptura*, the subject of this chapter.

What is this term *sola scriptura*, and why do we use it? This is a Latin phrase. *Scriptura* means (fairly obviously) "scripture"— the Bible. And *sola* means just that—"solely, only, nothing else." Hence in English we would say: scripture alone, the Bible alone, God's word alone. *Sola scriptura* is one of the so-called five *solas* of the Reformation. The others are grace alone, faith alone, Jesus Christ alone, and the glory of God alone. These are five essential truths of Christianity that were rescued, developed, and further defined during the great sixteenth-century struggle to return to the truth of Jesus Christ. It can even be argued that *sola scriptura* was the most important of these *solas*, because if we do not have the Bible as the source of truth, the one infallible touchstone, then we have nothing solid with which to determine the other truths!

We also must insist resolutely say that the Reformation *returned* to that truth. That is why we say that these five essential truths were rescued and developed at the time of the Reformation. In other words, as the title of this chapter indicates, the true church of the 1500s went back to a truth that had been held previously by the apostles and the apostolic church, but from which the church after the apostles had fallen. This doctrine of *sola scriptura* was not manufactured by the reformers five hundred years ago, but was set forth by God in the whole of his word and believed by the early New Testament church. Over the ensuing years, as the church sadly deformed, she fell away from the glorious simplicity of the gospel, and introduced heresy after heresy, this doctrine was also lost. It was inevitable that the apostate church of Rome would depart from scripture alone. Without this departure, she could not introduce her other false doctrines and wicked practices!

But it is also true that *sola scriptura* remains essential in the church today. God's truth is an unchanging truth, and all his truth remains vitally important in every age and place. It was vitally important in Isaiah's day. It was central during Christ's earthly ministry. Jesus continually appealed to scripture in support of what he taught (Matt. 4:4, 7, 10; 12:3; 19:4; 22:31; Luke 24:27). This truth was essential in the early church's proclamation of Jesus Christ as the fulfillment of all the Old Testament scripture. Consider all the quotations in the epistles. There are over seventy quotations of the Old Testament in Romans and over eighty in Hebrews. This truth was vital as the reformers battled to restore the gospel to the church, pruning away all Satan's evils introduced by Rome. It is no less vital today, in our warfare against Satan and the world, especially the cunning attempts of the false and apostate churches.

These are the things on which we will focus in this chapter. We will answer several crucial questions. First, what did the early church believe concerning scripture? Second, to what error concerning the Bible did the church succumb? Third, to what truth did the Reformation return? Fourth and finally, why is that truth still relevant for us today?

WHAT DID THE EARLY CHURCH BELIEVE CONCERNING SCRIPTURE?

When Jesus Christ ascended into heaven forty days after his resurrection, he had done so on behalf of the gathering of his New Testament church. During his earthly ministry he had called and equipped his apostles. He spent much time instructing them, demonstrating the fulfillment of the Old Testament scriptures through his words and deeds, and preparing them for what was to come (Mark 9:32; Luke 9:45; John 10:6). After his resurrection, Jesus continued to gather his church by the pouring out of the Holy Spirit on Pentecost. This pouring out of his Spirit and grace had as its purpose to enable his apostles and his people to obey his calling to preach the gospel in all the world. It was the calling to proclaim the truth of the kingdom of heaven, beginning at Jerusalem, and Judea, and Samaria, and going into all the world (Acts 1:8). This outpouring of the Spirit had as its purpose that the disciples would bring to mind all he had taught them. The Holy Spirit, according to his promise, would lead them into all truth (John 14:26).

The apostles, having received the gift of Christ in this way, were bold to preach the word. Those who had quavered and fled previously were now ready to lay down their lives as they declared the truth of Jesus Christ. Even the Sanhedrin were amazed, as they heard them speak and preach this word so boldly (Acts 4:13). By means of the word of God preached, thousands were added to the church (Acts 2:41; 4:4).

At the same time as the Holy Spirit was empowering the apostles to preach the scripture in all the world to the saving of thousands of God's elect, he was also inspiring holy men to finish writing the Bible. Holy Writ itself teaches that the apostles recognized that this was happening—scripture was being written. This is indicated by Peter, in 2 Peter 3:16, where he calls the writing of Paul "scriptures" and thus of equal authority to the other Old Testament writings. Therefore, by these men, the Holy Spirit wrote the inspired words of God. The remainder of the Bible was completed in the next sixty years, and the canon of scripture was closed by AD 95.

First Corinthians 13:10 says, "But when that which is perfect is come, then that which is in part shall be done away." Accordingly, when the Holy Spirit completed the work of that which is "perfect" (that is, the completed scripture), there would be no more need for that which was "in part." This refers to the special office of apostle and the special gifts of the Spirit such as miracles, tongue speaking, and prophecies. All of these disappeared, because there was no further need for them, now that God had given his word in its totality. By AD 100, the New Testament church had the completed scripture, one of the most amazing miracles of God, and one that we are able to hold in our hands and read every day! God specifically declared concerning those scriptures in Revelation 22:18–19:

> 18. For I testify unto every man that heareth the words of
> the prophecy of this book, If any man shall add unto

these things, God shall add unto him the plagues that are written in this book:

19. And if any man shall take away from the words of the book of this prophecy, God shall take away his part out of the book of life, and out of the holy city, and from the things which are written in this book.

But now we should ask the question: what did the early church believe concerning this completed book? We get a clear insight into what she believed (that is, their doctrine) by reading the preserved writings of some of the early church fathers.

Irenaeus (AD 130–202) was a bishop in Gaul who wrote extensively against errors that were already then arising in the church. He wrote: "We have known the method of our salvation by no other means than those by whom the gospel came to us; which gospel they truly preached; but afterward, by the will of God, they delivered to us in the Scriptures, to be for the future the foundation and pillar of our faith."[1] Thus Irenaeus clearly says that the gospel truth, the fullness of the life and salvation of Jesus Christ, came first of all by preaching. But then, he says, the Spirit caused that gospel truth to be written down (the scriptures), and that written word, he declares, is the future foundation of the church. Notice: not that which was spoken, but that which had been written, was the foundation of the church.

This raises an important issue. We all know about the game of telephone—when a message is relayed through multiple people it very often becomes distorted, sometimes markedly and amusingly. The early church faced a unique situation. Many in its midst

---

1 Irenaeus, *Against Heresies*, 3.1, quoted in Matt Slick, "Early Church Fathers' Quotes on Scripture Alone is final Authority," Christian Apologetics and Research Ministry, accessed February 28, 2018, https://carm.org/early-church -fathers-scripture.

had heard the apostles preach and teach, or perhaps they had heard the students of the apostles. They remembered with great clarity what had been spoken, and they were busy passing on to the succeeding generations the teaching and preaching they had heard. Sometimes this was doctrine, sometimes it was practical Christian living, or perhaps the orderly way of conducting worship in the church. What was the church to believe concerning such "tradition," the things that had been handed down, orally, from person to person in the church? What was to have the authority, scripture or tradition?

Cyprian (c. AD 200–258), a bishop at Carthage, wrote concerning a particular tradition (an orally transmitted teaching) that was being disputed.

> Whence is that tradition? Whether does it descend from the authority of the Lord and of the Gospel, or does it come from the commands and the epistles of the apostles? For that those things which are written must be done, God witnesses and admonishes, saying to Joshua the son of Nun: "The book of this law shall not depart out of thy mouth; but thou shalt meditate in it day and night, that thou mayest observe to do according to all that is written therein." [Josh. 1:8]…If, therefore, it is either prescribed in the Gospel, or contained in the epistles or Acts of the Apostles…let this divine and holy tradition be observed.[2]

Once again, it is very clear what the church's attitude was toward the scripture as it related to tradition. Although that which

---

2   Cyprian of Carthage, "To Pompey, Against the Epistle of Stephen About the Baptism of Heretics," 73.2, in Alexander Roberts and James Donaldson, trans. and ed., The Ante-Nicene Fathers, vol. 5, Fathers of the Third Century: Hippolytus, Cyprian, Caius, Novation, Appendix (Grand Rapids, MI: Wm. B. Eerdmans Publishing Company, repr. 1986), 386.

people had heard and understood from teachers of the past was important and worth considering, it was not the final authority for the church of Jesus Christ. What was important was this: "What saith the Lord in his written word?" The written word was what guided them in faith and life and that on which they stood firm against false tradition and error.

Athanasius (c. AD 300–375), bishop of Alexandria, was used of God to battle and defeat the Arians in their denial of the doctrine of the Trinity. He said, "The Holy Scriptures, given by inspiration of God, are of themselves sufficient toward the discovery of truth."[3] This word "sufficient" today often has the meaning of "just enough." This is not what it meant in Athanasius' day. Rather it had the idea of "everything necessary." It has this meaning, for example, in 2 Corinthians 12:9, where God said to Paul, "My grace is sufficient for thee." He meant that his grace would supply everything that the apostle needed to cope with his thorn in the flesh. That grace would not be just enough, but more than enough. By application, God's grace will also supply all that we need for the difficulties we face in our earthly lives. Thus, just as God's grace supplies everything necessary for us in our earthly lives, so it is that the ancient writers believed that the scripture was "sufficient." Nothing else was needful for the Christian's understanding, worship, walk, and life.

Athanasius also said, "The Catholic Christians will neither speak nor endure to hear anything in religion that is a stranger to Scripture; it being an evil heart of immodesty to speak those things which are not written."[4] Finally, after giving a list of the books of the New Testament, he said:

---

3 Athanasius, *Oration against the Gentiles*, quoted in Slick, "Early Church Fathers," https://carm.org/early-church-fathers-scripture.
4 Athanasius, *Exhort. ad Monachas*, quoted in ibid.

These are fountains of salvation, that they who thirst may be satisfied with the living words they contain. In these *alone* is proclaimed the doctrine of godliness. Let no man add to these, neither let him take ought from these. For concerning these the Lord put to shame the Sadducees, and said, "Ye do err, not knowing the Scriptures." And he reproved the Jews, saying, "Search the Scriptures, for these are they that testify of Me."[5]

This godly man would have nothing else but the scripture alone for faith and life.

Cyril of Jerusalem (c. AD 315–386) was a bishop and theologian. He was also involved in the training of students for the ministry of the word. In his lectures to them, he said:

Not even the least of the divine and holy mysteries of the faith ought to be handed down without the divine Scriptures. Do not simply give faith to me speaking these things to you except you have the proof of what I say from the divine Scriptures. For the security and preservation of our faith are not supported by ingenuity of speech, but by the proofs of the divine Scriptures.[6]

Notice Cyril's differentiation between "ingenuity of speech" and "*proof* of the divine scriptures" (emphasis added).

One final church father whom we ought to consider is Augustine (AD 354–430), bishop of Hippo and champion of orthodoxy against Pelagianism and semi-Pelagianism. In writing against these heresies, he appealed to the scripture to show their error.

---

5 Athanasius, *Festal Letter*, 39:6, quoted in ibid.
6 Cyril of Jerusalem, *Catechetical Lecture*, 4:17, quoted in ibid.

In order to leave room for such profitable discussions of difficult questions, there is a distinct boundary line separating all productions subsequent to apostolic times from the authoritative canonical books of the Old and New Testaments. The authority of these books has come down to us from the apostles through the successions of bishops and the extension of the Church, and, from a position of lofty supremacy, claims the submission of every faithful and pious mind...In the innumerable books that have been written latterly we may sometimes find the same truth as in Scripture, but there is not the same authority. Scripture has a sacredness peculiar to itself.[7]

Augustine insisted that the sacred scripture alone has authority in the church and in the lives of God's people. "Scripture has a sacredness peculiar to itself."

When we consider the church fathers, there is something significant to note. These men have been taken from a wide geographical cross-section of the ancient New Testament church, but they have also been chosen from a wide period of time: from the second to the fifth centuries. There is no doubt, across that wide cross-section, of the belief in the authority, the infallibility, and the sufficiency of scripture for faith and life. As contemporary theologian John Kelly says:

The clearest token of the prestige enjoyed by scripture is the fact that almost the entire theological effort of the fathers, whether their aims were polemical or constructive, was

---

7 Augustine, Reply to Faustus the Manichaean, 11:5, in Philip Schaff, ed., *The Nicene and Post-Nicene Fathers of the Christian Church*, 4 vols. *St. Augustin: The Writings Against the Manichaeans and Against the Donatists* (1887; repr., Grand Rapids, MI: Wm. B. Eerdmans Publishing Company, 1989), 4:180.

expended upon what amounted to the exposition of the Bible. Further, it was everywhere taken for granted that, for any doctrine to win acceptance, it had first to establish its Scriptural basis.[8]

In quoting this I do not mean to imply that you cannot find quotations from these same fathers that are loose and capable of alternative construction. Also, this understanding of scripture was not held by all theologians in all areas. But this is partly due to the fact that the church had not yet had to deal with many of the attacks against the doctrine of scripture that would later be launched by Satan and the apostate church of Rome. Hence it would only be much later, in response to these heretical attacks, that the true church and her theologians would be forced, by the good providence of God, to set down defined and creedal statements to which all would agree. In the meantime, the church was to undergo a great falling away into apostasy and error.

THE ERROR OF THE MEDIEVAL CHURCH OF ROME CONCERNING SCRIPTURE

With the Edict of Milan in AD 313, which legalized Christianity across the whole of the Roman Empire, persecution of the Christian church decreased markedly. But this had a negative effect also, for it meant that Christianity became somewhat popular, and many flooded into the church with little heart for the gospel of Christ. With this came many errors and a decline in commitment to the truth. The true church and godly theologians were forced to fight heresy on many fronts, such as the battles in which Athanasius and Augustine were engaged. From about AD 500,

---

8   J. N. D. Kelly, *Early Christian Doctrines*, 4th rev. ed. (London: Adam & Charles Black, 1968), 46.

there arose the increasing power of the bishop of Rome, who took to himself not only a power to rule in the church, but also a power and authority over secular matters. As the church conducted its "evangelism" it gained much in the way of material wealth, and many of the clergy took on roles of secular government and management. This culminated in the papacy and a system of hierarchy within the church, as well as a political kingdom that challenged the rights and authority of other secular kingdoms.

At the same time there arose the whole system of sacerdotalism: the priesthood of the church officers, who offered the sacrifice of the mass upon church altars. This became central in worship and participation in the mass was proclaimed indispensable for salvation. The people simply became the observers and recipients in Christian worship, and the "church" was seen as the pope and all the lower clergy. With this arose the doctrines of purgatory, worship of Mary and other saints, monastical orders and life, penance and the confessional, indulgences, and many other errors.

One might well ask, somewhat incredulously, "How did all these errors, which are directly contrary to the Bible, arise in the church?" It was because the doctrine of scripture itself became greatly corrupted. It was because the church of Rome turned away from the Bible as its sole rule of faith and life. Instead Rome herself became the rule for the church and what she would teach. In time, Rome became the false church who hated the truth of scripture and sought directly to destroy it, or keep it from the people.

That may seem like quite a bold statement. Can it be demonstrated? There is a multitude of evidences for this, but let us take up just two evidences for Rome's horrible descent into lies and error. The first evidence is the way in which she treated those who tried to use the Bible aright, thus showing her hatred for the truth.

The second evidence is her clear rejection of the ultimate authority and sufficiency of holy scripture.

For the first evidence, we turn to look at the life of John Wycliffe, who lived from approximately 1320 to 1384. According to the church historian Philip Schaff, Wycliffe's legacy was "his assertion of the supreme authority of the Bible for clergy and laymen alike and his gift to them of the Bible in their own tongue."[9] Wycliffe was used mightily by our Lord to begin to restore the Bible both to the ordinary believer and to the church.

Rome had removed the Bible in so many ways. In 1229 the Council of Toulouse made a decree forbidding the use of the Bible to laymen. Canon 14 declared: "We prohibit also that the laity should not be permitted to have the books of the Old or New Testament...we most strictly forbid their having any translation of these books."[10] The church only permitted the Bible to be read in Latin, and only the priests were allowed to have a copy of the Bible. Rome did not want anyone actually to know what the Bible said! We should also bear in mind that a very large number of Roman Catholic priests at that time were not only immoral and worldly, but were also illiterate.[11] Indeed, Wycliffe himself tells us that the "modern or recent doctors" of his time were pronouncing that parts of the Bible were "irrational, or blasphemous, or abounding in errors"![12]

Wycliffe came from a relatively affluent family, had a good education, and studied at Oxford University, where he eventually became a well-esteemed teacher. But as he studied the Bible, he

---

9   Philip Schaff, *History of the Christian Church* (1910; repr., Grand Rapids, MI: Wm. B. Eerdmans Publishing Company, 1952), 6:338.

10 Quoted in Edward Peters, *Heresy and Authority in Medieval Europe* (Philadelphia: University of Pennsylvania, 1980), 195.

11 Ibid., 6:662–63.

12 Ibid., 6:339.

became increasingly convinced that the church of his day taught much that was contrary to the scriptures. It was particularly toward the end of his life that he came to a clear understanding of many biblical truths and saw the importance of the scriptures. In 1378 Wycliffe published a paper entitled "On the Truth of Holy Scripture." According to church historian J. A. Wylie, "In this work he maintains 'the supreme authority of Scripture,' 'the right of private judgement,' and that 'Christ's law sufficeth by itself to rule Christ's Church.'"[13]

In this understanding, Wycliffe recognized the central importance of the people having the Bible in their own language and in their possession, in order that they might read, understand, and be blessed with the gospel. He therefore set about to do two things: to translate the Bible into the English language, and to train young men to go out and preach the gospel, taking with them portions of the word of God in the common language of the day. These young men were called "Lollards," a derogatory name given to them because of their speaking the gospel to all whom they met.

What was Roman Catholic hierarchy's response to this? Their response correlated exactly to their hatred for the truth of the scriptures. They did not want the truth of the Bible to go out to the people. Thus they opposed Wycliffe and his efforts to teach the people what the Bible said and get the scriptures into their hands and hearts. Initially they tried various ways of silencing him, but he was protected by his university status. Later, as he became bolder in his teaching against the papacy, Oxford deprived him of his position, but this enabled him to carry out his other activities of translation and training men to preach. He died of old age, teaching and preaching the truth of scripture top the end of his life.

---

13 J. A. Wylie, *The History of Protestantism* (London: Cassell Peter & Galpin, n.d.), 1:107.

But Rome was not finished with its hatred of Wycliffe and his teaching. Because of his stand for the truth, the Council of Constance declared him to be a heretic in 1415. Notice that this council was the same one that condemned John Hus and committed him to be burned at the stake for believing the same truths concerning scripture. This council excommunicated Wycliffe, banned his writings, demanded that they be burned, and ordered that his bones be dug up and burned. This highlights the depths to which the Roman church had sunk. She did not want the truth of the Bible to be known and would go to any lengths to prevent this. She could not have departed further from the early church's belief in scripture alone.

Then there is the second evidence—the evidence of clearly teaching the lie concerning God's word. For this evidence, we look at the declaration of the Council of Trent. The Council of Trent was a Roman Catholic council convened by Pope Paul III in 1546 in response to the Protestant Reformation. It issued condemnations of what it defined as the "heresies" committed by the Reformation and its doctrines. It is an excellent reference to understand all that Rome believed at that time.

After affirming the Apostles' Creed, the very first matter that the council took up was the doctrine of scripture. This immediately emphasizes to us that even Rome saw that this was a doctrine of immediate importance. The following is part of the Council's decree:

> Our Lord Jesus Christ, the Son of God, first promulgated with his own mouth, and then commanded to be preached by His Apostles to every creature, as the fountain of all, both saving truth, and moral discipline; and seeing clearly that this truth and discipline are contained

in the written books, *and the unwritten traditions* which, received by the Apostles from the mouth of Christ himself, or from the Apostles themselves, the Holy Ghost dictating, have come down even unto us, transmitted as it were from hand to hand: (the Synod) following the examples of the orthodox Fathers, *receives and venerates with an equal affection of piety and reverence,* all the books both of the Old and of the New Testament—seeing that one God is the author of both—*as also the said traditions,* as well those appertaining to faith as to morals, as having been dictated, either by Christ's own word of mouth, or by the Holy Ghost, *and preserved in the Catholic Church by a continuous succession.*[14]

This decree goes on to state that the books of the Bible include the Apocrypha. These books are necessary to the Roman Catholic Church in order to establish a number of her false teachings. They cannot be found in the true scriptures.

What can be ascertained from this positive declaration of Rome's teaching? First, the Council of Trent (and thus the Roman Catholic Church) puts scripture on an equal footing with the tradition that was held by the church and passed down from one generation to the next. Because the tradition was handed down (supposedly) from one generation to the next, in the "Catholic" (read "Roman Catholic") church, the only way properly to understand the scriptures was by holding, understanding, and applying that tradition. But of course, that tradition was only known and understood by those in "true succession" to the apostles: the

---

14 The Canons and Decrees of the Council of Trent, fourth session, "Decree Concerning the Canonical scriptures," in Schaff, *Creeds of Christendom,* 2:80; emphasis added.

priests who were ordained in the Roman Catholic Church and who maintained an absolute submission to the pope.

This means, second, that in all the doctrines to which Rome held (and still holds), she appealed to her own teaching, which is found in her "tradition." In the setting out of her doctrine, there are many appeals to her own theologians, and only an occasional reference to scripture. Where there are references to scripture, such references are always interpreted in the light of her own tradition and Magisterium.[15]

This was the situation that confronted the pre-reformers such as John Wycliffe and John Hus. It was also the situation that the leaders of the Reformation were to face later. It was impossible to take the Bible and use it to argue against the Roman Catholic Church, because she had a predetermined answer to any disagreements. Rome possessed the tradition, she had the Magisterium, and she had the pope. Thus everything she said was right, and what God said in his word was always reinterpreted in the "light" of Rome.

What did the reformers believe and teach?

THE REFORMERS' RETURN TO *SOLA SCRIPTURA*

The first of the reformers is Martin Luther, who began the events of the Reformation by nailing his Ninety-five Theses to the church door at Wittenberg. But Luther did not come to this point suddenly. Here was a man who, out of the fear and superstition bred into him by the Roman Catholic Church, devoted his life to serving God by becoming a monk.[16] He threw himself into his studies,

---

15 "Magisterium"—the official teaching of a bishop or especially the Pope.

16 Luther was caught in a violent thunderstorm while returning from visiting his parents in July 1505 and, fearing death, prayed to Saint Anna to preserve him, promising to become a monk. See Schaff, *History of the Christian Church*, 7:112.

but also into the life of physical self-denial and discipline: prayers, fastings, all-night vigils, and so on. He said later, "If ever...a monk got to heaven by monkery, I would have gotten there."[17] Despite all of this, he simply became more burdened. He gradually came to realize that he was unrighteous before a holy God and was under his wrath and curse.

But the Lord was gracious. Luther was also enabled to study the Bible and to begin to teach its truth. In the Lord's providence, he studied and taught his way through Romans and the Psalms. He came to the understanding, by God's grace and the light of the scriptures, that justification, and thus salvation, was by grace alone, by the righteousness of Christ alone, and received by faith alone.

What then were the Ninety-five Theses? They were occasioned by the hawking of indulgences in Luther's area of Germany by the Dominican friar Johann Tetzel. As Luther studied through Paul's epistles to the Romans, he became increasingly incensed by the obvious contradiction to the scripture of the church's doctrine and practice of indulgences. His biblical studies in the areas of sin, punishment, penance, forgiveness, and the indulgences being sold by the church resulted in these theses. They were assertions or conclusions derived from his study of scripture. These conclusions were opposed to the assertions found in the doctrines of the church. Luther did not wish to cause trouble and did not intend to stand up against the church. The purpose of his theses was debate. Luther wished to enter into earnest discussion of these matters, based on the scripture, so that either others could prove him wrong from scripture, or the church could be persuaded to become more conformed to God's word.

---

17 Ibid., 7:116.

Although it was not any new thing to post theses for discussion and debate, what Luther did was quite radical: to oppose the official doctrine and practice of the church based solely upon one's understanding of the clear statements of the Bible! This was indeed radical in those days. It was exactly what Wycliffe, Hus, and other men had done before. These men had been condemned, and many had been put to death by Rome as a result of their stand on scripture alone.

These actions of Martin Luther, clearly setting down the truths of scripture, and his growth in understanding the scriptures as he read, studied, and meditated on them, resulted in his development in the grace and knowledge of Jesus Christ. He taught, preached, and wrote much concerning the beautiful doctrines of salvation by grace, especially the liberating and comforting truth of full and free salvation in Jesus Christ. He emphasized justification by grace alone, through faith alone. Particularly Galatians 3:11 meant so much to him: "The just shall live by faith." Embracing these glorious truths in the Bible not only set him free from all the bondage and lies of the Roman church, but set his heart on fire to preach and teach to others these same truths from the scriptures. As Wylie puts it, "The Bible henceforward was to be to Luther the true city of God."[18]

But Luther's teachings also resulted in increasing consternation, condemnation, and hatred by the instituted church and especially the papacy. This was because Luther completely rejected the whole teaching of Rome regarding scripture *and* tradition. He especially rejected the teaching that tradition interpreted scripture. Evidence of this can be seen in the section "Concerning the Letter and the Spirit" in his treatise entitled "Answer to the

---

18 Wylie, *History of Protestantism*, 1:255.

Hyperchristian, Hyperspiritual, and Hyperlearned book by Goat Emser of Leipzig—Including Some Thoughts Regarding His Companion, The Fool Murner."[19] Here he sets out very clearly that he has abandoned as false the teaching of Rome and understands that it is the scriptures alone that are our rule of faith, and everything else must be judged by them.

> St. Paul says, in II Corinthians 4 [3:6], "The letter kills, but the Spirit gives life." My Emser uses and interprets this to mean that the Scripture has a two-fold meaning, an external one and a hidden one, and he calls these two meanings "literal" and "spiritual." The literal meaning is supposed to kill, the spiritual one is supposed to give life. He builds here upon Origen, Dionysius, and a few others who taught the same thing. He thinks he has hit the mark and need not look at clear Scripture because he has human teaching. He would also like me to follow him, to let Scripture go and take up human teaching. This I refuse to do, even though I too have made the same error. I intend, in precisely this example, to give reasons to show clearly that Origen, Jerome, Dionysius, and some others have erred and failed in this matter, that Emser builds upon sand, and that it is necessary to compare the fathers' books with Scripture and to judge them according to its light.[20]

Because of his forthright teaching and preaching the truth of scripture, the papacy determined that Luther had to be silenced, or Rome's whole kingdom of darkness and lies would be threatened.

---

19 Timothy F. Lull, ed., *Martin Luther's Basic Theological Writings* (Minneapolis, MN: Fortress Press, 1989), 74–103.

20 Ibid., 75.

Luther was summoned to appear before the Diet of Worms in 1527. Prior to this, Luther had refused to accede to the demands of Rome to stop or change his teaching. He had not responded to other summons to appear before the Roman councils or the pope. Indeed, on December 10, 1520, Luther not only had burned the papal bull against him, but had burned many other Romish books and documents.[21] The reason he attended this particular Diet was that he had been given a promise of safe conduct by the emperor, Charles V.

Luther came to this Diet prepared to discuss all of his teachings and writings in comparison to the scripture, and was even prepared to be shown from scripture where he was wrong. But to Luther's great disappointment, there was no opportunity to discuss his writings in the light of scripture. Rome had only one desire, and it most certainly was not to know and humbly submit to God in his holy word! It was to silence Luther and force him to submit to Rome's unbiblical lies and her temporal power.

At the Diet, Luther faced the emperor and all the might and pomp of the Roman Catholic rulers and theologians. He specifically asked, as he had done previously, to be shown from scripture where he was wrong, but this was refused. All of his books and writings were laid out before him, and he was asked to answer only two questions: "Are these your writings?" and "Will you recant and submit to Rome and to the pope?" His famous reply was:

> I cannot submit my faith either to the pope or to the councils, because it is clear as the day that they have frequently erred and contradicted each other. Unless therefore I am convinced by the testimony of Scripture, or by the clearest

---

21 Schaff, *History of the Christian Church*, 7:248.

reasoning—unless I am persuaded by the passages I have quoted, and unless they thus render my conscience bound by the word of God, *I cannot and I will not retract*, for it is unsafe for a Christian to speak against his conscience... Here I stand, I can do no other; may God help me! Amen![22]

This was a momentous occasion in the Reformation. Luther had spelled out exactly what all the other reformers would hold to also: that scripture alone is the rule on which the church and every believer must stand. By scripture alone they must judge the truth. Professor Lotz says:

Luther maintains that the word of God as gospel—as proclamation of God's gracious acceptance of sinners for Christ's sake—is the indispensable foundation, the *conditio sine qua non*, of the church's existence and of Christian faith and life. "One thing, and only one thing, is necessary for Christian life, righteousness, and freedom," he asserts in the *Freedom of a Christian* (1520). "That one thing is the most holy word of God, the gospel of Christ."[23]

As Jaroslav Pelikan puts it: "The primacy of the word of God was fundamental to the doctrine of the Reformation and to 'the whole substance of the Christian religion.'"[24]

This same understanding continued with all the other reformers. We cannot take the time to examine them all, but we ought

---

22 Quoted in J. H. Merle D'Aubigne, *History of the Reformation of the Sixteenth Century*, 5 vols., trans. H. White (1846; repr., Grand Rapids, MI, and New York, NY: Wm. B. Eerdmans Publishing Co. and The American Tract Society, n.d.), 2:265.

23 David W. Lotz, "Sola Scriptura: Luther on Biblical Authority," *Interpretation*, 35, no. 3 (July 1981): 261.

24 Jaroslav Pelikan, *Reformation of Church and Dogma (1300–1700)*, in *The Christian Tradition: A History of the Development of Doctrine*, 5 vols. (Chicago, IL: The University of Chicago Press, 1984), 4:187.

to demonstrate that this essential doctrine of *sola scriptura* was embraced by them generally.

I begin with Ulrich Zwingli (AD 1484–1531), pastor and theologian in Zurich, was a contemporary of Luther. Once again, as with Luther, it was studying the scripture that brought Zwingli to the truth. Indeed, as a Roman Catholic priest, he was converted under his own preaching. Peter Opitz says, "The decisive impulse of the Zurich Reformation was not a particular theological tenet or the religious experience of one single reformer. Rather, it was the discovery of the authority of scripture that was key."[25] The belief that Zwingli held concerning the Bible can easily be discerned from the confession he wrote, the Sixty-Seven Articles. Among these articles are the following:

1. All who say that the Gospel is nothing without the approbation of the Church, err and cast reproach upon God…

15. Who believes the gospel shall be saved; who believeth not shall be damned. For in the gospel the whole truth is clearly contained.

16. From the gospel we learn that the doctrines and traditions of men are of no use to salvation.[26]

We note here several important truths, including that the Bible is not subservient to the teaching or interpretation of the church, and that the scripture is sufficient for our salvation.

Heinrich Bullinger (1504–75) was a reformer, pastor, and the successor of Zwingli in Zurich. He was also the main author of the Second Helvetic Confession. This was adopted as the confession

---

25 Peter Opitz, "The Authority of Scripture in the Early Zurich Reformation," *Journal of Reformed Theology* 5, no. 3 (2011): 296.

26 Schaff, *Creeds of Christendom*, 1:364.

of the Reformed church throughout Switzerland. But it was also adopted by Reformed and Presbyterian churches in Scotland (1566), Hungary (1567), France (1571), and Poland (1578). In this confession, in chapter 1, we read:

> We believe and confess that the Canonical Scriptures of the Old and New Testaments are the true Word of God, and have sufficient authority in and of themselves, and not from men... They contain all that is necessary to a saving faith and a holy life; and hence nothing should be added to or taken from them.

In chapter 2 we read:

> We do not despise the interpretation of the Greek and Latin fathers and the teaching of Councils, but subordinate them to the Scriptures; honoring them as far as they agree with the Scriptures, and modestly dissenting from them when they go beyond or against the Scriptures.[27]

We notice in these writings of Bullinger that he defends both the sufficiency of scripture for all of faith and life, and also that its authority is found in itself, and thus it is the final authority to which all else must be compared. In other words: scripture alone.

The esteemed John Calvin (1509–64), reformer and pastor of Geneva, has multitudes of writings that touch upon the doctrine of scripture from which to demonstrate what he believed. We will restrict ourselves to his *Institutes of the Christian Religion*. Calvin points out that the scripture is inspired of God, "sprung from heaven," and has its authority from God, not from the church.

---

27 Ibid., 1:396–97.

In fact, the church has its foundation only in the scripture.[28] He then points out that the authority, clarity, and sufficiency of scripture are tied to the work of the Holy Spirit. He says that God "sent down the same Spirit by whose power he had dispensed the Word, to complete his work by the efficacious confirmation of the Word."[29]

Leaving the continental reformers, John Knox (c. 1505–1572), the great reformer of Scotland, possessed the same understanding of the Bible. This is not surprising, for he spent a good deal of time in Geneva between 1554 and 1559, studying under John Calvin. Knox was used of our Lord Jesus to bring the truth of the gospel most powerfully to Scotland, where it was readily received, by God's grace, among large numbers of the people and the nobility. However, the gospel and the clear declaration of scripture was opposed not only by the representatives of Rome, but also by the aristocracy and the reigning monarchs. Because of this, Knox had frequent discourses with the monarchs, especially with Mary, Queen of Scots.

Queen Mary, during one of those discussions, said, "Ye interpret the scriptures in one manner, and they in another. Whom shall I believe? Who shall be judge?" She was certainly not genuinely interested in learning the answer to this question. It was a way of deprecating Knox and all those who preached the truth, contrary to the Roman Catholic theologians. But John Knox answered very boldly and clearly:

Ye shall believe God, who plainly speaketh in his Word…
and farther than the Word teaches you, ye shall believe

---

28 John Calvin, *Institutes of the Christian Religion*, ed. John T. McNeill, trans. Ford Lewis Battles, 2 vols., Library of Christian Classics 20–21 (Philadelphia, PA: Westminster Press, 1960), 1.7.1–5, 1:74–81.

29 Ibid., 1.9.3, 1:95.

neither the one nor the other. The Word of God is plain in itself, and if in any one place there be obscurity, the Holy Ghost, who never is contrary to himself, explains the same more clearly in other places, so that there can remain no doubt but unto such as are obstinately ignorant.[30]

If there is anything else that could be said about this answer, it is this: Knox was not hesitant in speaking the truth! To call this powerful queen, who had already put to death a number of those who opposed her, one who remained obstinate in ignorance is quite something! But there is much more here. Knox clearly explains that the scripture, not Reformed or Roman Catholic theologians, is the sole authority in any debate regarding the truth. But he also maintains scripture's clarity and the Reformation principle that scripture interprets scripture. Knox understands and holds to the principle of scripture alone.

Examples could be multiplied to demonstrate this clear truth held across the whole gamut of the Reformation in many different countries. In fact, many of the reformers wrote papers or treatises on the importance and centrality of scripture because of the attacks of the Romanists on the one side and the radicals on the other, such as the Anabaptists and the mystics.

What can be said in summary of the reformers' teaching concerning scripture? It would be a monumental task to research all of the reformers and then carefully distill from all their writings, preaching, and teaching all that they believed concerning scripture. But the reality is that it is exceedingly easy for any one of us to find out what all these reformers, pastors, and theologians taught. In fact, we can know even more broadly what whole

---

30 Wylie, *History of Protestantism*, 3:503–4.

denominations of Reformed and Presbyterian believers teach concerning the doctrine of scripture.

This is because the whole Reformation movement understood the importance of recording very carefully the truth that was held and believed concerning God's word. They understood the importance of maintaining the "form of sound words" (2 Tim. 1:13), just as the ancient creeds of Nicea and Chalcedon formulated by the early church. Thus the reformers came to define the doctrines of the Reformation in various confessions and creeds. These were not only formulated and then adopted by the different Reformed churches throughout Europe, but they were also shared by these theologians and churches. The purpose of this sharing was to obtain from other Reformed and Presbyterian churches approval of and agreement with the doctrines contained in the confessions. For example, the French Confession of Faith was originally drawn up by the French Reformed churches, then sent to Calvin for review and editing. Theodore Beza and Pierre Viret also had input before it was finally adopted in 1559.[31]

Thus we can see exactly what the Reformed and Presbyterian churches believed, across the whole of the Reformation movement, and we can see that there is complete agreement among them. One significant example of this clear declaration of the truth of scripture alone is found in the Westminster Shorter Catechism. After declaring in question 1 that "Man's chief end is to glorify God, and to enjoy him forever," the catechism then asks in question 2: "What rule hath God given to direct us how we may glorify and enjoy him?" The answer is: "The Word of God, which is contained in the Scriptures of the Old and New Testaments, is the only rule to direct us how we may glorify and enjoy him."[32]

---

31 Schaff, *Creeds of Christendom*, 3:356.
32 Westminster Shorter Catechism 1–2, in ibid., 3:676.

After examining the confessions and creeds of the Presbyterian and Continental Reformed churches, we can summarize the biblical doctrine of scripture, to which the Reformation returned.[33] First, God teaches us in his word that the Bible is inspired. It is wholly and completely inspired, and thus *every part* and *every word* is the word of God (2 Tim. 3:16–17). At the same time, the sixty-six books of the Bible are the *only* inspired writings that God has given to his church (Luke 16:29; Eph. 2:20; Rev. 22:18–19). Arising out of this, of necessity, there are no errors at all in the Bible; it is inerrant and infallible (1 Thess. 2:13; 2 Tim. 3:16). Also of necessity, the Bible is authoritative. It is *the* authority over the individual and over the church (2 Pet. 1:19–21; 1 John 5:9). Indeed it is *the* authority over kings, presidents, and nations, regardless of whether they will acknowledge this or not (Ps. 2:10–12).

Next, they believed that the Bible is the only foundation of truth for all of faith and life. The beginning of wisdom is the fear of God (Prov. 9:10). The scripture is necessary for wisdom and for salvation. There is no other way that man can know God and come to salvation in Jesus Christ (Luke 16:31; Heb. 1:1–2). For this reason, the Bible is necessary. Without the scripture there is no wisdom, and there is no salvation (Prov. 22:19–21; Isa. 8:19–20; Matt. 4:4, 7, 10; Rom. 15:4).

The scriptures are also "sufficient"; in them is "everything necessary." This does not mean that every fact that exists is written down in the Bible, nor even that everything about God can be found there. John writes at the end of his gospel account, "And

---

33 The summaries of truth concerning the scriptures may be found in the following Reformed confessions: Westminster Confession of Faith chapter 1; Belgic Confession articles 2–7; Second Helvetic Confession chapters 1–2; Scots Confession chapter 19; the Thirty-Nine Articles VI–VII; French Confession of Faith sections II–V; Irish Articles of Religion 1–7.

there are also many other things which Jesus did, the which, if they should be written every one, I suppose that even the world itself could not contain the books that should be written. Amen" (John 21:25). But everything that we need to know about God, about salvation, and about the principles to guide us in every situation in life are found in the Bible.

The reformers' return to *sola scriptura* necessarily included a defense of scripture as "perspicuous." That scripture is perspicuous means that it is "clear" (Ps. 119:105, 130). The scripture is exceedingly profound and deep, and we cannot plumb fully the depths of it, but that does not mean that it is paradoxical or confusing. Very often today, those who wish to obfuscate the truth attempt to teach contradictory things from the Bible and wriggle out of their false teaching by calling it a "paradox."[34] By this they mean that particular teachings are contradictory to us, but with God, who is much higher than we are, these contradictions can be resolved. But our God is a God of order and not of confusion (1 Cor. 14:33). Thus scripture is always logical, orderly, and clear, even though it is more profound than we can comprehend. Scripture is so clear that even a child can know the scriptures from a young age as did Timothy (2 Tim. 3:15).

The reformers also contended that to understand the scriptures, men depended on the work of the Holy Spirit. The scriptures are spiritually discerned. But the Spirit and the word are never separated from each other (1 Cor. 2:9–14). Thus, God did not work anymore by revealing new truth to so-called "prophets," such as the Zwickau prophets of Luther's day contended. Rather,

---

34 There are two meanings of this word. One is simply a seemingly contradictory statement, but which can be resolved by further information or elucidation. But the second meaning is often meant by revilers of the truth of scripture: that of a truly self-contradictory statement.

the Holy Spirit works to reveal a right understanding of the clear, infallibly inspired, written, word of God.

In conclusion, the truth of *sola scriptura* was vitally important for the foundation and progress of the Reformation. In maintaining *sola scriptura*, the reformers held to the Rock of their salvation and the unchanging guide for their faith and life. They could be certain that they were speaking the truth because scripture plainly declared that truth, which the reformers then echoed. For this reason, many were content to die for the truth they taught and defended, thankful that God counted them worthy to suffer for the sake of Christ and for the gospel.

This also made the reformers' preaching and teaching powerful. Holding to *sola scriptura* meant that they preached and taught the doctrines of the word alone and not the commandments of men. The pure and clear truth of scripture, applied by the Spirit, resulted in large numbers of people who were saved out of darkness. God's elect heard the truth and voice of Christ speaking in his word, and hearing their Shepherd's voice, they came to him.

Sola scriptura also meant that the opponents of the Reformation were continually defeated. Rome and the radicals tried to marshal many arguments against the teachings of the Reformation, but the reformers responded by appeal to the Bible alone. This was sufficient to defeat all the wiles of the evil one and put to flight all the enemies of the truth. Trusting in the "sword of the Spirit," they were able to defeat "spiritual wickedness in high places" (Eph. 6:11–18).

THE RELEVANCE FOR TODAY

With the five hundredth anniversary of the beginning of the Reformation, a great deal of attention has been focused on this period of history. We might well ask: What is the point of talking and writing about events of five hundred years ago? Is it all just a talk-fest for history buffs? That was a long time ago, and would there not be far more profit in talking about matters of relevance for today? If we believe that the Bible is the very word of God and as relevant for us today as when the Holy Spirit caused it first to be written, we ought to be reminded of what the word of God teaches. After all, it is scripture alone that ought to guide all our thinking.

In several ways, scripture teaches its abiding relevance. First, consider Ecclesiastes 1:9: "The thing that hath been, it is that which shall be; and that which is done is that which shall be done: and there is no new thing under the sun." God tells us that the same things that the church faced five hundred years ago, two thousand years ago, and even five thousand years ago will be the same matters that confront the church today. They will be dressed up in different ways and have their own unique facets, but there is nothing new under the sun.

Second, call to mind the very first words that Satan uttered in the Bible, in Genesis 3:1: "Yea, hath God said?" Have you considered the significance of these words? Right from the very beginning Satan has desired to overthrow the word of God, and it has been his intention ever since. There is nothing new under the sun, and Satan has simply become more clever and more determined to destroy the word with his lies and wiles (Rev. 12:17).

We ought also to apply what we read in 1 Timothy 4:1: "Now the Spirit speaketh expressly, that in the latter times some shall depart from the faith, giving heed to seducing spirits, and doctrines of devils." We live in the latter times! The Spirit speaks expressly to us. Are we watching carefully, that we are not led astray by the false doctrines of Satan, who hates the full-orbed truth of the Bible?

Finally, Peter warns in 2 Peter 3:16–17 that there are some things hard to be understood in the Bible, "which they that are unlearned and unstable wrest, as they do also the other scriptures, unto their own destruction." Then he says, "Ye therefore, beloved, seeing ye know these things before, beware lest ye also, being led away with the error of the wicked, fall from your own stedfastness." This same error concerning scripture, by which the church was led into the great darkness of the Middle Ages, continues to assault the church today. Do we know this? Are we so aware of this? Do we see and are we resisting and fighting against this error as it arises in our day? It is no new thing that Satan is trying to overthrow the scripture, and it is no new thing that men arise who twist and pervert it by bringing in all manner of wrong ideas and philosophies. We must learn from the Reformation that the central truth of *sola scriptura* is vital to salvation, to faith, to life, to everything!

But the truth of *sola scriptura* is even more relevant in our twenty-first-century context. Are you aware that Roman Catholicism is still the most powerful so-called "Christian church" in the world today? About 50 percent of those who call themselves "Christian" in today's world are Roman Catholics; they comprise 16 percent of the world's population. But Rome still believes exactly what she did at the time of the Council of Trent, when she condemned and put the reformers to death. She hates the truth concerning *sola scriptura*. This is demonstrated in the *Catechism of the Roman Catholic Church*, last published in 1992:

> The Church...*does not* derive her certainty about all revealed truths *from the holy Scriptures alone. Both Scripture and Tradition* must be accepted and honoured with equal sentiments of devotion and reverence...

The task of giving an authentic interpretation of the Word of God, whether in its written form or in the form of Tradition, has been entrusted to the living teaching office of the Church alone…*This means that the task of interpretation has been entrusted to the bishops in communion with the successor of Peter, the Bishop of Rome.*[35]

Rome still reserves the right of the pope and her Magisterium to interpret what the Bible says about anything. What is more, Rome's truth is derived equally from "Tradition." That tradition cannot be found written down in any one place. Even what constitutes tradition, valid tradition, is determined by the Roman Catholic Church itself.

Besides the large number of professing Roman Catholics, about 25 percent of those who call themselves Christian in the world today are committed Pentecostals or charismatics? What is their take on the scripture? You will find that most Pentecostal churches pay lip service to the inspiration and authority of the Bible. For example, in the Assemblies of God 16 Fundamental Truths, number one is: "The Scriptures, both the Old and New Testaments, are verbally inspired of God and are the revelation of God to man, the infallible, authoritative rule of faith and conduct."[36] We would say: "Amen!"

However, the major focus of the Pentecostal churches is on the so-called "work of the Holy Spirit," which includes tongue-speaking, the interpretation of those tongues, and the acts of prophecy. As Frederick Bruner says, in his extensive work on the Pentecostal

---

35 *Catechism of the Catholic Church* (Washington, DC: United States Catholic Conference, 1994), 26–27(emphasis added).

36 "Assemblies of God 16 Fundamental Truths," The General Council of the Assemblies of God, accessed October 5, 2017, https://ag.org/Beliefs/Statement -of-Fundamental-Truths#1.

movement, "Prophecy is usually defined, even by the more careful in the Pentecostal movement, as something more than simply Spirit-inspired utterance, but as in fact the voice of the Spirit himself: in prophecy, we are told, we have 'the *speaking* Spirit."[37] Thus, according to the Pentecostals, the Holy Spirit has further revelation that is "fresh" and directly from God. Who could possibly take the two-thousand-year-old Bible and argue against that?

Often among Pentecostals there is a relatively poor knowledge of the Bible or of doctrine as a whole. They cling to certain passages of the Bible which they believe validate their peculiar beliefs, but their Christian life rests mainly on the emotional highs of their "Spirit-works" and "Spirit-words." The careful study and systematic setting forth of "all the counsel of God" (Acts 20:27) from the scriptures is neglected. They are blown about with every wind of doctrine (Eph. 4:14) that comes forth from their false "revelations of the Spirit."

But there is even more against which the church must contend today. Christians live in a culture, a society, and an environment in which Satan is attempting to overthrow, even within conservative churches, the authority, clarity, and sufficiency of the word of God. This is the modernism and postmodernism that is steadily creeping, unawares, into our churches (Jude 4).

Modernism teaches that if anything is old, it is outdated and needs to be changed and adapted to modern times make it useful. Applied to the word of God, modernism teaches that the Bible itself, and anything of the way that people used to think about the Bible, is no longer relevant nor useful. If these things are to be relevant and useful, each person and each church must take these

---

37 Frederick Dale Bruner, *A Theology of the Holy Spirit: The Pentecostal Experience and the New Testament Witness* (Grand Rapids, MI: William B. Eerdmans Publishing Company, 1970), 142.

things and update them, change and adapt them, so that they can be used in wonderful new ways. Thus we are told that we need to adapt the Bible and adapt Reformation doctrines and confessional statements so that they are new and actually useful to our contemporary setting.

The postmodern conception goes even further and says that there really is no such thing as objective, unchanging truth at all, and therefore there are no objective, moral values. Everything is relative, and what may be true for you is not necessarily true for me. Applied to the scripture, postmodernism says that the Bible cannot be taken to teach absolute truth and that the Bible can even be discarded, and it really does not matter. What matters is one's own reality inside one's self, and how one chooses to interpret the world and the Bible. The Bible can be useful, but only insofar as it is interpreted through your own personal reality. Therefore, many professing Christians can be heard to say, "Your interpretation is not necessarily my interpretation. What this scripture passage says to you is not necessarily what it says to me." Thus there is no way for the church or anyone to determine what the Bible actually teaches.

Both modernism and postmodernism are in direct opposition to the truth that God sets forth in scripture. There is nothing new under the sun. Satan is once again saying, "Yea, hath God said?" The modern-day church is listening and giving heed to the doctrine of devils. This is why the modern church is going off in many different directions with all sorts of new teaching, contemporary worship, and social welfare projects. The modern church is content with man's theory of evolution and the evil teaching of the homosexual movement. Scripture is no longer the guide for what we believe and how we live. We are no longer anchored to the word of God. What God says in scripture is no longer the all-sufficient, infallible rule of faith and life.

We must see that *sola scriptura* is not just an interesting historical note, nor only just an important matter for five hundred years ago. May we be convinced that our immutable, covenantal God has given to us his unchanging truth in the inspired scripture. Do we see that it is still important to insist on *sola scriptura*? Do we see that it is still as vital for the church to uphold, maintain, and defend this truth today as it was for the reformers? Are we still convinced that it will be increasingly important to continue holding firmly to this truth and applying it practically, as we witness for the glory of the gospel of Jesus Christ and await his coming on the clouds of glory?

We must never submit to the church alone. The sad deformation of the church during the Middle Ages occurred because the people simply submitted to what the visible church declared and taught, not to what God said in the Bible. It is to scripture alone that we must go in order to learn what a true church of Jesus Christ looks like, and then commit ourselves to be such a church. Then we will also listen for and hear the beautiful truth of our Savior preached in her midst. Then we will receive the word with all readiness of mind and search the scriptures daily, whether those things are so (Acts 17:11). We will hear the voice of our Savior and gladly submit to it and follow after it. That is the blessing of scripture alone.

May we grow in our love and appreciation for the word of God and our determination to know it, depend on it, and defend it. May *sola scriptura* be the glad and determined declaration of our hearts and our churches. In that way we will truly commemorate the anniversary of the Reformation.

Chapter 3

THE CHURCH FINDS HER VOICE AGAIN: THE REFORMATION DOCTRINE OF THE PRIESTHOOD OF ALL BELIEVERS
(God's Renewed Answer to a 3,500-Year-Old Prayer)

Barrett L. Gritters

≈

Would God that all the Lord's people were prophets,
and that the Lord would put his spirit upon them!
—Numbers 11:29

The doctrine of the priesthood of all believers, rediscovered and restored at the Reformation, changed the lives of the people of God dramatically. The church found her voice again. In other words, believers learned again of their right to speak truth and were taught how to speak truth. What the church had received at Pentecost and then lost over the course of a millennium was restored to her. She learned how to read scripture, how to understand scripture, how to educate in the faith of the Bible.

71

Then, based on this newly learned scripture, ordinary Christians gained the ability to judge what the church was teaching. They were now qualified to discern what was truth and what was error, and thus leave the church teaching error and join the church (or establish a new one) that was faithful to the scriptures they had studied.

The doctrine of the priesthood of all believers, therefore, most irritated Rome. It was the greatest threat to the Roman Catholic hierarchy. The Reformation taught the common believer how to think critically again. Then it gave to common believers the right to voice their objections.

It is not surprising that some scholars have suggested that the principle of the priesthood of all believers is the main principle of the Reformation.[1] Others, only slightly more modest in their estimation of the principle, give it pride of place among what they judge to be the three major principles: *sola scriptura*, justification by faith alone, and the priesthood of believers. Another suggests, intriguingly, that the "sum" of the *solas* of the Reformation is the priesthood of all believers. Add up the *solas*, he suggests, and one gets the priesthood of believers. "As the Reformers expounded these three truths [*sola scriptura*, *sola fides*, and *sola gratia*] they found themselves proclaiming the doctrine of the priesthood of believers."[2]

Although Luther might not be found making such bold assertions for his principle, no one can argue that he did not consider

---

1   Kevin J. Vanhoozer says, "I referred to the priesthood of all believers as the final principle of mere Protestant Christianity—that is, the end and purpose of salvation history," in *Biblical Authority after Babel: Retrieving the Solas in the Spirit of Mere Protestant Christianity* (Grand Rapids, MI: Brazos Press, 2016), 155.

2   Cyril Eastwood, *The Priesthood of All Believers: An Examination of the Doctrine from the Reformation to the Present Day* (Minneapolis, MN: Augsburg Publishing House, 1962), 241.

this to be a doctrine of first-order magnitude.[3] This is the judgment of Timothy George, as he indicates in a 2016 *First Things* web-exclusive post:

> Another cardinal principle of the Reformation was the priesthood of all believers. In his *Address to the Nobility of the German Nation* (1520), Luther criticized the traditional distinction between the "temporal" and "spiritual" orders—the laity and the clergy—arguing that all who belong to Christ through faith, baptism, and the Gospel shared in the priesthood of Jesus Christ and belonged "truly to the spiritual estate": "For whoever comes out of the water of baptism can boast that he is already a consecrated priest, bishop, and pope, although of course it is not seemly that just anybody shall exercise such office."[4]

It is striking that this critical doctrine finds so small a place in the corpus of Reformation creeds. Except for two brief mentions, and in neither case explicit or full bodied, the Reformed confessions are almost silent on the subject. There is nothing in the Belgic Confession or Canons of Dordt and nothing in the Westminster Confession or Catechisms.

There are two brief creedal references. Only one of them makes the doctrine official for Reformed churches.

The Swiss reformer Heinrich Bullinger's Second Helvetic Confession names believers as priests. "The apostles of Christ do term all those who believe in Christ 'priests,'... because that all the

---

3   See, for example, Luther's "To the Christian Nobility of the German Nation Concern the Reform of the Christian Estate," in *The Christian in Society*, in *Luther's Works*, 44:127.

4   Timothy George, "The Priesthood of All Believers," *First Things*, The Institute on Religion and Public Life, October 31, 2016, accessed November 27, 2016, https://www.firstthings.com/web-exclusives/2016/10/the-priesthood-of-all-believers.

faithful, being made kings and priests, may, through Christ, offer up spiritual sacrifices unto God."[5] Yet Bullinger's expression of this grand doctrine is muted, even weak, mostly because it was not his intent to establish this doctrine in his creed. First, it appears not in a section dealing with the believer, but in the section on the ministers of the gospel. When explaining that the office of the gospel minister is not a "priesthood," the Second Helvetic qualifies that denial, saying, so to speak: "It is true that all believers have been made kings and priests, but the ministry is not another priesthood as Rome sees it." Second, even when the priestly office is mentioned, only offering up spiritual sacrifices is mentioned as the duty of the believer as priest. Third, Bullinger says nothing of the prophetic and kingly tasks of the believer. Important confessional reference, indeed, but not nearly a satisfactory expression of the doctrine. Besides, the Second Helvetic is not an official creed of most Reformed denominations today.[6]

The Heidelberg Catechism, arguably the great pearl of Reformed confessions, is the only major Reformed creed to give Reformed churches the doctrine of the priesthood of all believers in positive, clear, and creedal form. How thankful, therefore, Reformed churches ought to be for the Heidelberg Catechism!

> Question 31. Why is he called *Christ*, that is, *Anointed*?
> Answer. Because he is ordained of God the Father, and anointed with the Holy Ghost, to be our chief Prophet and

---

5 Second Helvetic Confession, "Of the Ministers of the Church, Their Institution and Offices," in Schaff, *Creeds of Christendom*, 3:879.

6 In its beginnings, the Second Helvetic Confession *was* officially adopted by many Reformed churches in Europe—both in eastern and western Europe—and by every canton in Switzerland except Basel. Elector Frederick III commissioned Bullinger to write the creed shortly after he commissioned the Heidelberg Catechism. See James T. Dennison Jr.'s introduction to the Second Helvetic in his *Reformed Confessions of the 16th and 17th Centuries in English Translation*, vol. 2 (Grand Rapids, MI: Reformation Heritage Books, 2010), 809–881.

Teacher, who fully reveals to us the secret counsel and will of God concerning our redemption; and our only High Priest, who by the one sacrifice of his body, has redeemed us, and ever liveth to make [continual] intercession for us with the Father; and our eternal King, who governs us by his Word and Spirit, and defends and preserves us in [the enjoyment of] the redemption obtained for us.

Question 32. But why art *thou* called a Christian?

Answer. Because by faith I am a member of Christ, and thus a partaker of his anointing; in order that I also may confess his name, may present myself a living sacrifice of thankfulness to him, and may with free conscience fight against sin and the devil in this life, and hereafter, in eternity, reign with him over all creatures.[7]

But even the Heidelberg does not confess with the strength and clarity that we in the twenty-first century could wish for. Although it gives to believers the functions of the three offices and by that implies that all believers are prophets, priests, and kings, the creed does not explicitly say that Christians hold the threefold office.

The calling of Reformed believers in our day is, therefore, while appreciating the value and beauty of the Heidelberg's confession, both to recognize how the church since the Reformation developed the truth confessed in it and then to see to it that the doctrine is not lost again! If the Reformed church today is not on her guard, she will lose this fundamental truth again. There is evidence that the church's hold on it is not strong.

There are certainly threats to the five *solas* about which Reformed churches must speak. But I would propose that there

---

7 Heidelberg Catechism Q&A 31–32, in Schaff, *Creeds of Christendom*, 3:317–18.

are deadly threats—very practical and real threats—to the teaching that every believer holds the threefold office of prophet, priest, and king. These threats are not often as quickly noticed as the threats to the *solas* might be.

When I spoke on this subject to two large audiences of Reformed believers at Reformation 500th anniversary celebrations in 2017, I asked how many of them held office in their local church. Even though they were aware that the doctrine I was to expound to them was the doctrine of the priesthood of all believers, most were caught off guard and did not raise their hands, except, not surprisingly, those in the special office of elder, deacon, and minister. Of course, it was a trick question. "Holding office"—the phrase I used in conducting the informal poll—is usually a description of what elders, deacons, and ministers are privileged to do. I intended, however, to make every believer present at the meeting—men, women, and children—realize that each one of them held office in their church. Because each one professed to be a believer, each one was a prophet, priest, and king. Everyone should have raised a hand.

The fact is, trick question or not, they should not have been caught off guard. Every catechized believer—even fourteen-year-olds in Protestant Reformed churches have been trained for two years in the Heidelberg Catechism—should be able to detect the question for the trick it was. Every catechized believer should be able immediately to say, "I am an officebearer in the church. I hold office in my local congregation."

THE DOCTRINE OF THE PRIESTHOOD OF ALL BELIEVERS

Simply put, this is the Reformed doctrine of the priesthood of all believers: because Christ is anointed by God to be God's chief officebearer, and because all believers "partake" in Christ's anointing, all believers are officebearers under Jesus Christ. Because Christ's office is the threefold office of prophet, priest, and king, the believer's office is also threefold: he is prophet, priest, and king.

This is the Heidelberg Catechism's teaching in Lord's Day 12 (see above). First, the catechism teaches that God anointed his Son, Jesus. Jesus is "ordained of God the Father and anointed with the Holy Ghost." In his eternal decree, God ordained Jesus to this position under him. God chose Christ to be the Officebearer. Then, at Jesus' baptism, God anointed him with the real anointing of the Holy Spirit. In this way, Jesus was installed into the office of our "chief Prophet and Teacher," our "only High Priest," and our "eternal King." At his baptism, Jesus became the Christ, the Messiah, to whom all the Old Testament prophets pointed.

This explains Jesus' choice of text for his first sermon in his hometown of Nazareth. When Jesus went to the synagogue on the sabbath day, Luke 4 says that the scroll of the prophet Esaias was delivered to him. "And when he had opened the book, he found the place where it was written, The Spirit of the Lord is upon me, because he hath anointed me...And he began to say unto them, This day is this scripture fulfilled in your ears" (vv. 17–18, 21). Jesus announced publicly that he was the Christ, the Anointed of God.

Then the Heidelberg Catechism asks, "Why art thou called a Christian?" Believers answer with the beautiful confession, "Because by faith I am a member of Christ, and thus a partaker of his anointing."[8] Following this, the Catechism gives the functions and responsibilities of prophets, priests, and kings. Thus, even though it does not explicitly name believers as prophets, priests, and kings, that is the clear implication.

---

8 Heidelberg Catechism Q&A 32, in ibid., 3:318.

The catechism's teaching is biblical. What God prophesied in Exodus 19:6, "Ye shall be unto me a kingdom of priests," he fully granted in the new dispensation. In the first epistle of Peter, the word of God to the church is, "But ye are...a royal priesthood" (1 Pet. 2:9). The New Testament church is the fulfillment of God's Old Testament kingdom. The church, with all her members, is the royal priesthood. God "made us kings and priests" unto himself (Rev. 1:6). What God had prophesied also in Joel, "Your sons and your daughters shall prophesy" (2:28), he gave when the anointing Spirit was poured out upon "all flesh" in Acts 2:17.

To illustrate this coming New Testament reality, the Old Testament paints a striking picture in Psalm 133. When Aaron the high priest—type of Jesus Christ—was anointed with the sacred oil poured out upon his head, that precious ointment ran down his beard and then "down to the skirts of his garments" (v. 2). That is, the anointing that was given to the head, Jesus Christ, flows down upon his body and reaches down all the way to the skirts of his garments, to all the members of his body. All members of his body are anointed into offices under him.

A SPONTANEOUS BUT GOD-INSPIRED PRAYER

What the Old Testament prophesied was also the subject of a relatively obscure prayer that Moses offered in Numbers 11. There, Moses had groaned to God about the heavy burden of the complaining multitude of Israel, especially the "mixed multitude" (v. 4) among them. "Moses...was displeased" (v. 10) and vented this to God. "I am not able to bear all this people alone, because it is too heavy for me" (v. 14). Instead of rebuking Moses, as we might expect, God promised him seventy officebearers to help him, precursors of the New Testament elder. God would "take of the spirit" that was on Moses and would "put it upon them" (v. 17), thus qualifying the seventy to do the work that, until now, only Moses had been able to do.

This grand anointing was to take place at the tabernacle, where the seventy were to gather, God informed Moses. In fact, only sixty-eight of the seventy assembled. Two, Eldad and Medad, for some unknown reason remained "in the camp" (v. 26). But the spirit that the sixty-eight received, enabling them to prophesy, fell also upon these two, and they prophesied.

When an overzealous young man reported this curiosity to Moses' servant Joshua, Joshua immediately advised Moses, "My lord Moses, forbid them" (v. 28). But Moses perceived matters better than his young understudy did and exclaimed, "Would God that all the LORD's people were prophets, and that the LORD would put his spirit upon them!" (v. 29). With the prophetic "Spirit of Christ" in him (1 Pet. 1:11), Moses prayed for the anointing of all the people of God, that all of them would function as prophets. He wished all Israel to have a voice.

It took two thousand years, but at Pentecost God answered Moses' prayer. God took of the Spirit that was upon Christ (typified by Moses), and he put it upon all the Lord's people—men and women, old people and young, educated and uneducated, rich as well as poor. He poured out his spirit on the whole congregation. All believers were anointed to office. They became prophets, priests, and kings, under Jesus, the anointed, the Christ.

Watch these Spirit-endued believers in Acts 2 and later. As prophets, they spoke the "wonderful works of God" (v. 11) because the Spirit of Christ in them enabled them to understand what, days before, they did not understand. Bold as lions, these newly crowned kings defended the faith, fought against sin, even laid down their lives in behalf of God's name. Priests all, they devoted themselves to the cause of living with God. Sheltered consciously in the blood of the Lamb once sacrificed, they lived in God's presence and sacrificed themselves, especially in the cause of missions, in which these believers led others into God's covenantal love that they knew. They were prophets, priests, and kings.

A LOST VOICE RECOVERED

In a process so gradual that few who lived through it noticed, the church lost that voice Christ's Spirit had given her. She lost the truth of the priesthood of believers and the practice of the three-fold office she had once engaged in. Gradually, indeed. Over the course of 1,500 years!

The once-pure but now-corrupt church obscured the truth that every believer was an officeholder by virtue of baptism and faith. Then the apostate church robbed the people of their right and privilege to know the scripture; to read it became contrary to church law. The common people were completely dependent on the Roman Catholic priesthood. Blindly they were to assent to the teaching and rule of the clergy. If they wanted personal access to their Father in heaven, they found themselves two or three steps removed from him. First, they must find a father-priest, who then might point them to the mediatrix Mary, who would pass on their requests to the too-majestic and therefore distant mediator Christ, so that in this way he might bring their petitions to the triune God.

Eventually the poor people lost their prophetic voice. Their kingly arm atrophied. Their priestly heart went cold.

Their voice was lost until, that is, the Lord restored this truth to his church especially through the teaching of Luther. The Heidelberg Catechism's teaching was the doctrine reclaimed by Luther. Luther said, "All Christians are truly of the spiritual estate...for baptism, gospel, and faith alone make us spiritual and a Christian people...We are all consecrated priests through baptism."[9]

Luther was objecting to the Roman Catholic teaching that there are two kinds of Christians: the "spiritual estate" comprised of the clergy—priests and bishops, cardinals and popes; and the "secular estate" comprised of all others—laborers and farmers, lawyers and bankers, children and mothers. "All Christians are truly of the spiritual estate...We are all consecrated priests through baptism."

Immediately, Luther's teachings bore fruit. He made the Bible available to all, written in their own language, understood even by the plowboy. He made the pulpit the focal point of public worship and the sermon its central activity—in the vulgar tongue that everyone could understand. Under Luther's influence, commentaries proliferated, enabling young and untrained preachers to make good sermons and believers to search the scriptures more thoroughly.

The doctrine that Luther and other first-generation reformers confessed, Calvin affirmed. "In him we are all priests...to offer praises and thanksgiving, in short, to offer ourselves and ours to God."[10] Calvin repeatedly carried the tradition of Luther further. Among many other of Calvin's contributions to the Reformation, I mention only one of his greatest: the institution of the public, weekly Bible study, where not only the ministers, but interested laypeople took turns explaining and applying scripture. One

---

9   Martin Luther, "Address to the Christian Nobility of the German Nation", *The Christian in Society*, in Luther's *Works*, 44:127. Luther maintained this biblical doctrine in the face of the challenge presented by the "enthusiasts" who took it to an extreme. They rejected the special offices altogether and then made the priesthood doctrine a license for interpreting the Bible according to the dictates of one's own conscience, making way for "interpretive anarchy" in the church. For more on this, see Vanhoozer, *Biblical Authority after Babel*, especially chapter 4.

10   Calvin, *Institutes*, 4.19.28, 2:1476.

former Italian bishop reported his observations of a visit to Calvin's Bible study:

> Every week, on Fridays, a conference is held in the largest church in which all their ministers and many of the people participate. Here one of them reads a passage from scripture and expounds it briefly. Another speaks on the matter what to him is according to the Spirit. A third person gives his opinion, and a fourth adds some things in his capacity to weigh the issue.[11]

In the sovereign and good providences of God, 3,500 years after Moses first made his prayer, and 1,500 years after it was first answered, God answered Moses' prayer again. The church found her voice again.

POSITIONS OF SERVICE

Before showing how this doctrine of the priesthood of believers is threatened, it is appropriate to acknowledge how rich it is for the Reformed believer, and why some consider it to be the heart of restored Reformation doctrine.

At the outset, and what makes the teaching very rich, it must be noted that receiving an office is not so much receiving a position of honor, but taking on a responsibility to labor. On behalf of the God who appointed him, the officebearer works, even toils. Jesus Christ's office gave him honor, indeed. But more so, it assigned to him lifelong labor for God, strenuous, self-denying labor to the death. So with every officebearer today: he is not in the office for honor but for service. When Eldad and Medad received some of the Spirit from Moses, they did not parade themselves among the people as worthy of esteem but immediately

---

11 Quoted in VanHoozer, *Biblical Authority after Babel*, 159–60.

began serving, prophesying among the people, willingly helping sinful people with personal problems so numerous and marriage contentions so difficult that Moses could not bear them. But working together with Moses, the seventy elders would serve to assist the congregation in their difficulties. When the Spirit anointed the one hundred and twenty on Pentecost, they did not strut haughtily among the crowds of onlookers, boasting of their new position, but began serving, speaking to all and sundry the "wonderful works of God" (Acts 2:11). Ministers minister, just as their redeemer Christ, who came not to be ministered unto but to minister (see Matt. 20:28).

For believers today, their office of service may well lead them to be martyred for their prophetic witness, literally burned on the altar of their offering of themselves to God, and slaughtered in their kingly battle to defend the faith of King Jesus. Christ promised his disciples as much. Right after he told them that he chose them and ordained them to go and be fruitful—to work—he reminded them that this service of Christ would lead to being hated, just as he was hated.

16. I have chosen you, and ordained you, that ye should go and bring forth fruit...

18. If the world hate you, ye know that it hated me before it hated you.

19. If ye were of the world, the world would love his own: but because ye are not of the world, but I have chosen you out of the world, therefore the world hateth you.

20. Remember the word that I said unto you, The servant is not greater than his lord. If they have persecuted me, they will also persecute you; if they have kept my saying, they will keep yours also. (John 15:16, 18–20)

Receiving the office of believer is not unlike receiving a special office in the church, of elder, deacon, or pastor. The naïve aspirant to the office of elder who imagines that he may gain some prestige in the congregation as an elder soon learns that the burden of the work and weight of responsibility far exceed whatever little honor he may gain. He dies for the God whom he serves. So it is also for those who serve Christ in the office of all believers.

THE FUNCTIONS OF EACH OFFICE: THE PROPHETIC OFFICE

What believers do in their threefold office needs careful explanation. A prophet's main calling is not to tell the future, even though foretelling may be included in his work. A prophet's work is to know and then to speak on behalf of God.

We start with the office of prophet, even though the Reformation's formulation is "the *priesthood* of all believers." The believer's office is called a priesthood, not to the exclusion of or in any respect a minimizing of the prophetic office, but because the priestly includes the prophetic. For this reason, when he was expounding the office of "priest," Luther was fond of quoting Malachi 2:7: "For the priest's lips should keep knowledge, and they should seek the law at his mouth: for he is the messenger of the LORD of hosts." Malachi 2, Luther wanted to remind the Roman Catholic priests, shows the prophetic nature of the priest's office—to know the word of God and teach it to the people. This calling of the priest to teach was well-known in the Old Testament. Teachers know truth; teachers speak truth.

Early in Old Testament history God made that plain. God promised, regarding the prophet, "I...will put my words in his mouth; and he shall speak unto them all that I shall command him" (Deut. 18:18). He warned that "the prophet, which shall presume to *speak a word in my name*, which I have not commanded him to speak…even that prophet shall die" (v. 20, emphasis added). The people of God expected the prophet to speak, sometimes about the future, but mostly about God and his will. The Samaritan woman at the well, some 1,500 years after Moses, knew this. "I know that Messias cometh…he will *tell us all things*" (John 4:25; emphasis added). According to his own confession in John 17, Jesus did tell them "all things" (v. 7) from God. Jesus "manifested thy [God's] name" to his disciples (v. 6); he gave "unto them the words" that God gave him (v. 8).

Thus, in their prophetic office, believers know and speak on behalf of God. The Heidelberg Catechism explains it this way. Believers know the truth because Christ "fully reveals to us the secret counsel and will of God concerning our redemption."[12] With that knowledge they can confess his name. Brief as the catechism's explanation is, the doctrine is present there in its essential elements: believers can know and do speak on behalf of God.

What was not fully spelled out in the confessions, and not fully explained by the reformers, may be more expansively told today.

All believers can know the secret counsel of God concerning their redemption. Little children can know truth. This is why the Reformed church begins teaching the children catechism at age five or six, and parents read scripture to them at even younger ages. The perspicuous scripture is open to them, and their understandings, Spirit illumined as they are, are open to the scripture. High-school-aged youth can study the deep doctrines of God's word for four years in catechism and then honestly confess that they believe "all the doctrines contained in the Old and New Testaments and in the Articles of the Christian faith and taught here

---

12 Heidelberg Catechism A 31, in Schaff, *Creeds of Christendom*, 3:317.

in this Christian church to be the true and complete doctrine of salvation." These knowledgeable prophets can even vow to "adhere to this doctrine" and "reject all heresies repugnant thereto."[13] Why? Because they can know God's truth.

Knowing the truth, believers can confess the truth. Young parents, without degrees in theology, can teach their children the truth of Jesus Christ. This begins in family worship where the father usually presides, but also involves bedtime devotions where the mother may read a Bible story and apply it to her toddler's life. Before the children leave for school, the mother may read a psalm or proverb and lead the children in prayer for their day ahead. John Knox, great Scottish reformer, called for this application of the office of all believers. He exhorted all the men in his congregations, "Ye be in your own houses bishops and kings…let there be worship of God morning and evening."[14]

All Christians, young or old, can also prophesy throughout the day, declaring the "wonderful works of God" (Acts 2:11) in the workplace or asking their neighbor to listen to "what he [God] hath done for my soul" (Ps. 66:16). For this reason, evangelism committees of local congregations can include members who are not in the special office of prophet (pastor). Although these non-ordained members do not preach, they can participate in their congregation's witness in many ways.

Closer to home, every believer has the competence to counsel other believers. Such is the testimony of Paul in Romans 15:14:

---

13 Public Confession of Faith: Questions and Answers, in *The Psalter with Doctrinal Standards, Liturgy, Church Order, and added Chorale Section*, reprinted and revised edition of the 1912 United Presbyterian *Psalter* (Grand Rapids, MI: Wm. B. Eerdmans Publishing Co., 1927; rev. ed. 1995), 59.

14 Quoted in E. Gordon Rupp, "The Age of the Reformation: 1500–1648," in *The Layman in Christian History*, ed. Stephen Charles Neill and Hans-Ruedi Weber (Philadelphia, PA: The Westminster Press, 1963), 145.

"And I myself also am persuaded of you, my brethren, that ye also are full of goodness, filled with all knowledge, able also to admonish one another." Notice the order: first filled with knowledge; then able to teach.

The prophetic office of believer is never seen more clearly, however, than in the weekly public worship of the congregation. What had not happened for generations before the Reformation now began again: the congregation participated in worship. And one of the main ways in which the congregation participated was by singing. The prophesying in song that was done *for* them by the priests now was done *by* them. They recognized their priestly right to offer up "sacrifice[s] of praise to God continually, that is, the fruit of [their] lips giving thanks to his name" (Heb. 13:15). For this reason, Reformed churches historically have avoided choirs in public worship—not only because they feared the return to Rome's practices, but especially because they cherished and defended their privilege to prophesy!

So important is this prophetic function in public worship that by singing ordinary believers even participate in the mutual instruction of the members. In public worship! This is surprising, but it is the teaching of Ephesians 5:19 and, especially, of Colossians 3:16. With the "word of Christ" dwelling in them richly, the believer's singing is an act of instruction, of "teaching and admonishing one another." In the congregational singing of scripture (the "psalms and hymns and spiritual songs" refer to the 150 psalms of David) all believers are exercising their prophetic office of teaching, in public worship. Believers must listen to this instruction. They must consciously prophesy when they sing. "I will sing with the spirit, and I will sing with the *understanding* also" (1 Cor. 14:15, emphasis added).

This prophetic calling also explains why, in many Reformed

churches' public worship, the believers in unison recite the Apostles' Creed. This belongs to what the Heidelberg Catechism describes as confessing his name.[15] In harmony with the Reformation's desire that believers participate in as many aspects of public worship as possible, the minister does not confess faith for them, but with them. From the heart and with the mouth, believers confess.

Another dimension of the prophetic calling is to judge truth and right in the congregation's life.[16] Because they know truth and righteousness from their study of scripture, believers can judge truth and right. Believers judge the minister's sermons (his prophesying to them in his special office of preacher). They also judge the elders' government of them (their ruling of them in the special office of elder).

The full implications of this calling were recognized only gradually as the Reformation progressed. But already early in the Reformation's progress, believers themselves judged the teaching of indulgences evil, the worship of Mary idolatry, the fear of purgatory unfounded. They learned again the nobility of the Bereans and searched the scripture to see if what they were taught was true (Acts 17:11). They could also judge whether the church's demands for Christian living were biblical; whether trips to the confessional, abstinence from meat on Fridays, celibacy for certain classes of members, and more were truly the righteousness required of believers in the Bible. Then, as kings, believers had the right to protest, to fight and to oppose error. Common believers were growing in the knowledge of truth!

---

15 Heidelberg Catechism A 32, in Schaff, *Creeds of Christendom*, 3:318.
16 Judging, as well as protesting, are aspects also of the kingly office; but we treat them in part here, recognizing that the offices, though distinct, cannot be separated. The prophet's calling sometimes demands kingly exercises.

One man described the situation, as early as 1522, in this way: "Recently I heard a matron who was able to discuss the relation between Law and Gospel in the Epistle to the Romans more learnedly than many of our great doctors." Another, in 1537, thus: "The lay people do now know the holy scripture better than many of us, and the Germans have made the text of the Bible so plain and easy with the Hebrew and the Greek that now many things be better understood without any glosses at all than by all the commentaries of the doctors."[17]

Believers were finding their voice again!

FUNCTIONING IN THE PRIESTLY OFFICE

Believers are also priests, whose calling is to draw near to God, come into his presence, offering sacrifices that honor him. Included in the work of a priest is to bring others to God. First, his highest and ultimate priestly calling is to draw near to God.

The Heidelberg Catechism explains it this way: Christ, the chief High Priest, by the one sacrifice of his body, has redeemed us and makes continual intercession with the Father for us. We, priests under Christ, now present ourselves living sacrifice(s) of thankfulness to him.[18] Also in this case, the doctrine of the priesthood of believers is expressed, but only minimally.

The priest's main and ultimate calling at the time of the Reformation was to offer a bloody sacrifice. But this sacrificial task is easily misunderstood and thus the priest's essential calling not fully appreciated. The church must not limit the description of the priest's work to offering sacrifice. It is necessary to see the bloody sacrifice in its context. So I repeat: the priest's central calling was

---

17 Quoted in Rupp, "The Age of Reformation," in Neill and Weber, *The Layman in Christian History*, 143.

18 Heidelberg Catechism A 31–32, in Schaff, *Creeds of Christendom*, 3:318.

to bring the people to God, to lead them, as it were by the hand, into God's house and his fellowship.

Watch the Old Testament priest perform his office. When he approaches God, he cannot enter God's house directly. Sin bars him from entering. Even though God lives right among the people, shows himself to them in his glory in the tabernacle, they cannot enter. Sin is the great barrier to their way into fellowship with him. The elaborate ritual God required of the priest before he could enter the tabernacle—centered in the sacrificial offering—was designed to show the people how the barrier of sin could be removed. To make simple what at first appears to be complex, an offering must be made to atone for sin. Only then, with the justice of God satisfied, could the priest enter God's house and fellowship with him. His calling, at heart, was to enter into God's presence—by way of a sacrifice.

The priest did not, however, enter God's presence alone. With him, the priest brought the whole congregation into God's chamber. The congregation was represented by precious stones on his shoulders (as a heavy burden) and more precious stones upon his breastplate, on his heart (as objects of his love). The priest took the people into the presence of God, into God's bed chamber, to be loved and to love. There the God of all glory received the adoration of his blood-bought bride, his sister, his spouse (Song of Sol. 4:10).

Understood in this context, the sacrifice offered by the priest is a means to the highest end—the end being sweet fellowship with God. The priest sacrificed, indeed. But he sacrificed only to accomplish his main task: bringing God's people into his fellowship and love.

Now, turn your attention to Jesus Christ, priest. Watch him perform his priestly work. The people God gave him were in trouble, separated from God by their sins, unfit for fellowship with the holy God on account of their filth. See Christ come down from heaven to do the work of priest—devoting himself to God in perfect holiness, spotless himself of any stain. See him walk the way to the altar of the cross with the burden of his people's sins on his shoulders and love in his heart. Watch the Lamb be slain, not for his own sins, but for the sins of those whom God gave him. Then, having shed his blood as atonement, see him ascend into the "holiest" presence of God, where he intercedes for his people. He pleads his own blood, clothes his people with his own righteousness, and gives them access to the Father through his own work.

That is, Christ's priestly work was not finished at the cross but continues in his daily intercessions for us and continual sanctifying of us. He "ever liveth to make intercession" for us (Heb. 7:25; see also Rom. 8:26, 27, 34). In his tender love and priestly mercy (Heb. 2:17), he redeemed us by his own blood and now daily brings us into his Father's presence.

His work not yet finished, in heaven Christ turns around, raises his hands, and says, "The Lord bless thee, and keep thee: the Lord make his face shine upon thee, and be gracious unto thee: the Lord lift up his countenance upon thee, and give thee peace" (Num. 6:24–26). Now too, as priest, he sanctifies us, preparing us for a place in heaven, and in heaven a place for us—in the presence of his Father. Behold him "sanctify" (wash) his people by his truth (John 17:17).

Beautiful Savior! If the high priests in the Old Testament were beautiful in all their garments, how much more beautiful is not our Lord Jesus as our priest! He brings us to God!

This explanation not only helps clarify, but also enriches the understanding of the task of believers as priests. If we would limit the task of the believer to offering sacrifices, even sacrifices of praise, important as these are, it would not do justice to the right and privilege all believers have! They have the right and privilege to come into the very presence of God—as priests. The reformers understood this, even if it is not spelled out in the confessions with the clarity one might wish. The reformers made very clear to the people of God their right to confess their sin, seek forgiveness, and obtain pardon, without the work of a human priest.

Every believer has priestly access into the secret and sweet presence of God himself. Of course, they pray only in the name and merits of Christ, whose bloody sacrifice gives them the right to enter. But even the littlest children with the most immature faith, perhaps even when father and mother are long asleep in the dark of night, even they have the ability and right to cry out, "Come close to me, Father; I am afraid!" Or, "Forgive my sins, for Jesus' sake!" God gives ear to the cries of these little priests, like so many Samuels. He comes to them, fellowships with them, speaks by his Spirit into their little hearts, and enables the child-like faith of these priests to conclude, "I will both lay me down in peace, and sleep: for thou, LORD, only makest me dwell in safety" (Ps. 4:8).

What we lost through priestly Adam in paradise, priestly Christ restored to us by his sacrifice: sweet, personal fellowship with God, the ability to walk and talk with our friend. We can go to him and speak to him, face to face. With a boldness that far exceeds that of the Old Testament high priest, ordinary Christians may "enter into the holiest by the blood of Jesus" (Heb. 10:19).

The believer does not need the minister to take him to God, even though he may ask his pastor for help in a time of deep distress. The Christian does not need to wait for an elder to pray for him, even if at times he feels like his prayers do not rise more than an inch above his head. "For through him [Jesus Christ] we both have access by one Spirit unto the Father" (Eph. 2:18).

But deep distress is often the lot for the believer. The deep distress is that he feels God to be far from him, an experience "more bitter than death," as the Canons of Dordt say.[19] In these times, the believer is reminded that his remedy must be to draw near to God. Sometimes a caution is necessary for Christians when the billows go over him: do not seek improper remedies for your distress. But more necessary is the encouragement the distressed need to hear: "God is approachable through Jesus Christ. You are a priest who may come to him without fear. Enter into the holiest by the blood of Jesus, and find acceptance there. No matter how undeserving you are—and you are—he is pleased to have you come. Come! Your priestly privilege is to go directly to God, in the name and merits of Jesus Christ. You may love him and be loved."

A second important aspect of the believer's priestly task is leading others into God's presence. Believers intercede for their fellow members, thus bringing other believers into the presence of God. Parents lead their little ones to Jesus in prayer. Parents and grandparents plead with God for their children and grandchildren, sometimes because these dear family members are wayward. God hears these priestly intercessions made in the name of his Son.

Priests even lead unbelievers into God's presence. The prophetic witness of believers to unbelievers is a priestly act. We point the unbeliever to the way into the holiest: trust in Christ the only sacrifice for your sin. When believers love their neighbor in this way, truly pitying him in his misery of unbelief, we reflect our "merciful...high priest" (Heb. 2:17) who pitied us in the misery

---

19 Canons of Dordt 5.13, in ibid., 3:595.

of our unbelief. Following Christ, we pity our neighbor by calling him to repentance and faith in the same Christ whom we trust.

Third, the priestly work of believers manifests itself in the office of deacon, the ministry of mercy. Just as the prophetic office of believers appears also in the special office of gospel preacher, so the believer's priestly office appears also in the special office of deacon. A large part of believers' mercy toward the suffering is expressed through the benevolence of the church, administered by the deacons. The financially needy receive our gifts, which we give to the benevolent (poor) fund. We must promote and protect the office of deacon in the church today, lest we dishonor Christ's own priestly ministry of mercy through the deacons.

All this must not be taken to mean that the Heidelberg Catechism and the Second Helvetic Confession are mistaken, or even weak, when they call upon New Testament priests to offer "a living sacrifice of thankfulness to him"[20] and "offer up spiritual sacrifices unto God."[21] Sacrifice is a major aspect of our priestly calling, for the central offering that the believer offers as priest is the offering of himself. As priest, he places himself on the altar of consecration to God. Although this offering is called a "living" sacrifice to distinguish it from the atoning offering that only Christ could make, this offering of himself to God today is a real sacrifice, a dying to one's self. As the believers in the Old Testament gave up their possessions in their worship at the tabernacle, believers in the New Testament give up themselves. We offer everything to God.

This is Paul's teaching in Romans. The "reasonable service" of Christians today is that they "present [their] bodies a living sacrifice, holy, acceptable unto God, which is your reasonable

---

20 Heidelberg Catechism A 32, in ibid., 3:318.
21 Second Helvetic Confession, "Of the Ministers of the Church," in ibid., 3:879.

service" (Rom. 12:1). This is the full-time work of believers today. A man or woman today who claims to be a believer but does not offer himself or herself to God gives the lie to his or her claim. It may not therefore be said that believers are only permitted to offer ourselves to God, or only have the right to come into his presence; it must be taught that Christians must do this.

The final note here demands more than a footnote: No small part of the priestly work of Reformed Christians today is to battle for the Reformed truth of Christ alone, that is, in his priestly offering for sin. This Reformed *sola* (*solus Christus*) first forbids the believer to imagine that any sacrifice that he makes in any respect makes payment for any sin that he has committed. That payment is offered alone by the Priest, Jesus Christ. Second, it demands of the believer to do (kingly) battle against every teaching that proposes supplements to the priestly work of Christ or proposes any assistant to him in his payment for our sins. To say more here would require another chapter. But it must be said: priests that we are, we will not allow the great High Priest, Jesus Christ, to be dishonored in that way.

FUNCTIONING IN THE KINGLY OFFICE

The last of the three offices is king. Believers all are kings. Because Jesus Christ is king and we partake of his anointing, we are kings.

The Heidelberg Catechism says Christ is "our eternal King, who governs us by his Word and Spirit, and defends and preserves us in the redemption obtained for us."[22] We, kings under Christ, "with free conscience fight against sin and the devil in this life, and hereafter, in eternity, reign with him over all creatures."[23] With the sword of the Spirit in their hand and mouth, believers are kingly

---

22 Heidelberg Catechism A 31, in ibid., 3:318.
23 Heidelberg Catechism A 32, in ibid.

in their conduct. They have the right and ability to be active in the government, defense, and preservation of Christ's kingdom.

This aspect of believers' calling is rich and diverse. Its breadth is not often recognized. Reformed Christians today have the calling to explain kingship, defend kingship, even develop it more fully.

The believer's kingly activity must not be limited to the battles he fights against sin. The Catechism's mention only of "fight[ing] against sin and the devil in this life," although proper, does not go far enough. The Christian's kingly calling includes governing. His governing labor is not only the rule he exercises over his own possessions, but also government in the church. In a very significant way, every believer participates in Jesus Christ's royal government of his kingdom in the church.

Begin, however, with the duties Christians have outside the official life of the church. Christians rule their own property, their own bodies, spirits, and souls. Each believer has his or her own little kingdom that requires careful government. She rules her own body well as to sexual purity, exercise, diet, and rest. He asks King Jesus to put a guard at the door of his lips (Ps. 141:3) because he who refrains his lips is wise (Prov. 10:19). She controls her temper because that's more honorable than taking a city (16:32). Christian students manage their time carefully, because even time belongs to King Jesus. The whole of the Christian life can be described in terms of the Christian functioning as king, both governing himself and doing battle against sin and Satan in himself. When he understands the monumental task he has in his private life, he hardly dares look for more kingly responsibilities outside his private life. But there are more—many more.

When a young man and young woman marry, they take on the new and greater responsibility of exercising kingly rule in their home and fighting against sin there. If the Lord blesses them with children, their kingdom's realm becomes even wider and immeasurably more difficult. Other Christians must govern the kingdom of the business the Lord provides them, and maybe a multitude of employees. Rule well! Govern wisely! Judge fairly! Fight bravely! You are kings under Jesus Christ.

Rule in the church must also have our attention, however. Here the church must be loud and clear in her instruction to her members. Believers, young and old, participate in the government of the church of Christ. That starts by acknowledging that the church's government is most directly exercised through the elders. Theirs is the office of rule. Elders stand at the forefront in the fight against sin and Satan in the church. Christ puts the church's government in their hands. If the church as kingdom can be compared to a civil kingdom, elders are responsible for the judicial, the legislative, and the executive branches of government.

First, elders explain and interpret the law of God revealed in scripture. Second, they are permitted, within strict limits, to make laws, to "establish certain ordinances" for "maintaining the body of the Church." The Belgic Confession, whose language this is, cautions that when the elders formulate regulations for the church, they "do not depart from those things which Christ, our only master, hath instituted," and that, positively, they aim at only "that which tends to nourish and preserve concord, and unity."[24] But elders make laws. Third, elders exercise discipline over those members (even over themselves) who disobey King Jesus by their confession or walk. In this work, the elders declare those who are impenitent to be outside of the kingdom of God.

It will be helpful to compare this kingly office to the other two offices. Believers exercise their office of prophet largely through the voice of the minister, their office of priest largely through the

---

24 Belgic Confession 32, in ibid., 3:423.

hearts and hands of the deacons, and (now) their office of king in a significant way through the elders. Then, as is true with the other special offices, if our church's elders are not doing their work, or doing it contrary to Christ's will, our kingly calling is hindered. Our duty then is to act. It is not to wring our hands or to immediately find another church. Instead, we respectfully but quickly call the erring elders to their responsibilities. As kings, all believers must act against any dishonor of King Jesus by the special office of elder.

However, believers exercise royal government and kingly dominion beyond the rule of their own lives and more than through their elders. Significant as these are, they are not all that New Testament believers do as kings. They also participate in the rule and government of the church herself. They take an active part in the kingly government of the church.

To speak clearly, believers do not merely observe the church being ruled, they participate in the rule. So important is this rule by ordinary believers in the church that some have claimed that this is the fundamental rule in the church. I do not judge it to be the fundamental rule, but the believer's role is certainly crucial.[25]

Believers have a voice in the government of the church. They participate in the election of officebearers by suggesting names of candidates, by approving the names put forward by the council,

---

25 Herman Hanko, "Notes on the Church Order" and "The Believers' Manual For Church Order," unpublished syllabus (Grandville, MI: Theological School of the Protestant Reformed Churches, n.d.). The two parts are paginated separately. The quotations are from the second part, pp. 3, 4. Hanko says that the special offices are the "outgrowth" of the believers' office, that the special offices "proceed out of" the believers' office, that the "most fundamental office is that of believer," that "the fundamental authority of Christ exercised in the church is held by believers," "the office of believers is the basic office in the church," and that "final authority...rests in the office of believer." The reader will have to judge for himself whether this is indeed the hyperbole that I judge it to be.

and by actually choosing them by majority vote at a congregational meeting. This is rule in the church, which explains why in Reformed churches historically women have not voted at the congregational meetings.

Also Christian discipline, which may lead to final excommunication, is rule in the congregation. Discipline is King Jesus fighting against sin within. According to Jesus' own instructions in Matthew 18, this discipline often begins not with elders but with the ordinary members. Only after the private admonitions of the member are resisted does the matter come to the elders, and then it is brought there by the member himself.

Discipline then continues, according to the Reformed church order, with the whole congregation participating in the impenitent's public discipline. They hear the series of announcements (Titus 3:10) made by the elders that call the members to pray for the member under discipline or seek him out to admonish him. If these acts bring no repentance, all the members of the local church assemble in a public worship service (1 Cor. 5:4) to put the impenitent member out. This public excommunication is then confirmed and carried out practically when the members of the church keep no company (vv. 9, 11) with the member, with the hope that he becomes ashamed and repents (2 Thess. 3:14). Even though the elders are "front and center" in these actions of Christian discipline, all believers exercise kingly rule in it.

Finally, believers exercise their kingly office when they present objections to the teachings or conduct of the church that they judge to be improper. If, according to scripture, the confessions, or the church order, the church has taught or acted improperly, believers not only may but must exercise their kingly office and fight against the error. When a row ensues, the objector must not be accused of troublemaking but praised for an act of holy warfare. In this act, believers combine the prophetic office of speaking truth with the kingly office of fighting against error.

Reformed church orders that have roots in Dordt's church polity (1618–19) explain the right of this kingly act for believers. "If anyone complain that he has been wronged by the decision of a minor assembly [consistory or classis], he shall have the right to appeal to a major ecclesiastical assembly."[26] "Anyone" refers to any member in the church. Most have understood this to refer to confessing believers, either men or women. Men and women bring their complaint as an "appeal" to a major assembly. Implied is that they have already brought their objection to the minor assembly and have not convinced the minor assembly of the error that they allege. They are all kings in Christ's church and function in a kingly way.

The Reformed church order reflects a rich understanding of believers' participation in the government of the church, and by that it carries even further the Reformation's understanding of the kingly office believers hold.

THE REAL DANGER OF LOSING OUR VOICE AGAIN

What an honorable place the Lord gave again to believers in his church through the Reformation. The church found her voice once more. She must not lose it again.

But there is a real danger that she does. None must harbor hope that the devil is uninterested in this pearl of great price that believers possess. He wants to rob us of it. Thus our Reformation celebration may not be a self-satisfied celebration of a possession

---

26 Church Order of the Protestant Reformed Churches 31, in *The Confessions and the Church Order of the Protestant Reformed Churches* (Grandville, MI: Protestant Reformed Churches in America, 2005), 390.

to which we are only loosely holding. It is indeed possible for the church to lose her voice again, for her spiritual muscles to atrophy, and for her priestly hearts of consecration to grow cold or inactive.

It is worth repeating that, if the church loses this office and work, she will also lose the *solas*. She can lose the office by misuse or abuse of it, in a multitude of ways. I mention only a few.

Using our office for selfish advancement and self-promotion is abuse of the office. It should not be surprising that this warning comes first. Both in the Old Testament and New, early in church history and late, men in office allowed their sinful natures to turn the office from an office of service to an office of self-service. How many prophets, priests, and kings in Israel's day were not self-servers, and how often was not Israel chastised for allowing it to be so? Churches today who defend the office must do so by constant reminders that the purpose of the office is to serve others.

Abuse of the office takes place when believers speak prophetically but not from scripture or rule as kings but not on the basis of God's word. God's kings wield one sword, the sword of the Spirit, which is the word of God. The Old Testament's warning about false prophets applies today too: "He shall speak...all that I shall command him...But the prophet, which shall presume to speak a word in my name, which I have not commanded him to speak...even that prophet shall die" (Deut. 18:18, 20). No more than a preacher may speak from the pulpit his own opinion may a believer declare as from God except on the basis of scripture. Under the judgment of God, the office will be lost again.

Misuse of the office could take place if the office is over-esteemed. In fact, this abuse has occurred, even if not often, in close proximity to Reformed churches. But one significant branch of the Reformation so emphasized the office of believer (wrongly so) that they rejected the special offices. These were the Anabaptists. Their heirs today have every man preach and no body of elders that truly rules the congregation.

Related to this is the misuse of the office of believer by those who imagine that they can learn, study, and know the word of God apart from the communion of saints, both now and in the past. Luther called this radical, religious individualism. No one may read, interpret, and prophesy divorced from the community of faith today and from the cloud of witnesses of the past. "The spirits of the prophets are subject to the prophets. For God is not the author of confusion, but of peace" (1 Cor. 14:32–33).

But the greater danger of losing the office is by non-use. Not by abuse but by non-use. The people of God become ignorant of the word. They do not read the Bible and good literature at home. They do not attend and therefore do not prepare for Bible studies. The men who ought to be leaders allow the women this position by default. Then the only readers are the women; the women's Bible studies are well attended but not the men's. Thus the warning: do not lose your voice by non-use!

Or parents neglect to use their prophetic voice in teaching their children. They allow everyone else to speak the word of God to their children, but they do not. The Christian school teachers do such a fine job that the parents are inclined to abdicate their position as the primary educators of their children. The ministers teach catechism so thoroughly that the parents are tempted not to give any biblical instruction to their children themselves. When the instruction of the children is given over to the experts, parents begin to see themselves as unimportant and, soon, incompetent. Thus the warning: do not lose your voice by non-use!

Or if a protest should be lodged because the church embraces false doctrine or the elders allow ungodly living, members must protest but do not, giving one excuse or another. Or if another member falls into sin, he should be confronted as Jesus teaches in Matthew 18, but everyone thinks someone else will take up the onerous task. The hope that someone else will write the protest or confront the fallen neighbor is understandable but must be resisted. The prophetic voice is lost if it is not used. People of God, do not lose your voice by non-use!

IN CONCLUSION: AVOIDING TRAGEDY

How does a church avoid such tragedy? Only if, by the grace of God, she is committed to teach and train and exhort her members to use their prophet's voice, exercise their king's arm, and keep a healthy heart of mercy. Teach. Train. Exhort. Without this, the voice will be lost again.

First, not any member may speak. Only those who know the word of God may speak prophetically. Not just anyone may protest, but only those who ground their objections on scripture and the confessions. Not just anyone may call unbelievers to Christ with a priestly pity, but only those who know how properly to describe the Christ to whom they must come. The church who would maintain her voice must teach her members.

To accomplish this, the elders will be determined that the sermons are doctrinal, that is, instructive. They will want their members to leave the worship exclaiming, "I learned from the word of God today!" The old Reformed tradition of catechism instruction for children from earliest days until confession of faith will not be lost. In that catechism, the children learn not only the truth of scripture, but also the proper way to use their voice, to wield the sword in the congregation if necessary, and to live as merciful high priests.

Ah, to have such a church of which I am member!

It is one thing for us to learn what rights and privileges were restored at the Reformation. It is another thing for all of us to see to it that we and our generations are and remain qualified to exercise those rights and privileges.

Strong men who wickedly and forcefully remove the office from the people is one danger. Another is that the people, pathetically, hand it over to them by sloth and negligence.

We have a great treasure in the truth of the priesthood of believers. The high and holy privilege to serve under Christ is ours and our children's. It is a calling for everyone to take up. Let us be faithful to God in maintaining the truth that God restored to the church at the Reformation.

"Would God that all the LORD's people were prophets, and that the LORD would put his spirit upon them!" (Num. 11:29).

Chapter 4

THE REFORMATION'S RECOVERY OF RIGHT WORSHIP

Martyn McGeown

≈

*I was glad when they said unto me, Let us go into the house
of the LORD. Our feet shall stand within thy gates, O Jerusalem.*

—PSALM 122:1–2

Worship is one of the highest expressions of covenantal life with our God. When we come together for worship, we appear before our God as his people to bring to him our praise, thanksgiving, and adoration. When we worship, especially in public worship, we come to hear what our God will say to us. God speaks to us chiefly through the preaching of the gospel, and we respond to him through singing, prayer, confession, and the giving of our offerings.

The Reformation restored right worship. This was necessary because worship had been corrupted. When the people came to worship God, barriers had been erected, which made the worship of God difficult, if not impossible. Those barriers still exist, to a large degree, in the worship of the Roman Catholic Church today. The barriers are, first, idolatry; second, incomprehensibility; and third, a lack of congregational participation. The reformers, in different ways and to different degrees, dismantled those three barriers and restored worship to the biblical pattern: "God is a Spirit: and they that worship him must worship him in spirit and in truth" (John 4:24).

What did a typical medieval worshiper experience when he entered his local parish church for worship? Imagine coming to your place of worship on Sunday and experiencing this.

First, he met a priest, whom he revered as a mediator between God and man. The priest brought the medieval worshiper into the presence of God. Without the priest, no worship was possible. The Reformation restored the priesthood of all believers, thus dispensing with the need for priests or for a special priestly class in the church.

Second, he encountered a liturgy that was almost entirely in a foreign language. The average medieval worshiper was illiterate: he often could not read or write his own language, and he certainly could not read or write in Latin, which was not only the international language of scholarship, but also the language of the church. In fact, a good number of the priests were illiterate and could barely speak Latin. Therefore, they recited the liturgy that they had learned with barely more comprehension than the worshipers before them. Sermons, if they existed, were short homilies, which consisted of myths about the saints or wild allegories, with barely any explanation of the text of the Bible and no setting forth of the gospel of grace.

Third, he encountered an ornately decorated building, for since the people were illiterate, the church deemed it best to teach the people by means of images, which were seen as "books for the laity."[1] The images of Jesus, Mary, and the saints, as well depictions

---

1   Heidelberg Catechism Q 98, in Schaff, *Creeds of Christendom*, 3:343.

as of biblical events (such as the last supper, the crucifixion of Jesus, and the final judgment), were idols before which the people would bow and to which the people would pray.

Fourth, the worshiper was very much a spectator to the awesome drama of the mass. The pulpit was not front and center; the eucharistic altar was front and center. The medieval layman believed that the priest could change or transubstantiate the bread and wine of the mass into the very body, blood, soul, and divinity of the Lord Jesus Christ, which transubstantiated elements were then worshiped as God. The ordinary worshiper sat awestruck before the mystery of the mass but understood little of what was transpiring before his eyes. When the time came for him to partake of the mass, he received only a small wafer on his tongue, while the church withheld the wine from him.

Fifth, the worshiper was not permitted to participate in any meaningful way in the worship service. Even singing was the task of professional choirs. A medieval worshiper, therefore, was a curious spectator of a divine mystery in which he had no meaningful part.

In such a liturgical setting, there is no fellowship with God, there is no hearing from God, there is no edification, and there is therefore no true worship. The church in its deformation had robbed the people of God of the worship of God. Besides that, since the late medieval church had lost the gospel, the people had no reason to worship God. They came to worship out of fear, rather than out of thankfulness for the gracious salvation that God had given in Jesus Christ.

We can divide the responses of the reformers to this into three main categories. First, Luther's revision of the liturgy was light and even superficial, for liturgical revision was not Luther's emphasis. He was more concerned with the doctrine of justification by faith alone. While he tore down some of the liturgical edifice that Rome had erected, he did not expend much effort in rebuilding the worship of God according to the biblical pattern.

Second, the Swiss, especially Zwingli, took a more radical approach. In a way, the followers of Zwingli "threw the baby out with the bathwater." They not only removed choirs and organs, but also prohibited congregational singing![2] (Obviously, I do not mean to classify Zwingli as "radical" in the sense of the Anabaptists, which is an altogether different degree of radicalism!)

Third, Calvin worked mightily to restore the worship of the church to a strictly biblical pattern. Calvin especially developed the regulative principle of worship, something unheard of in Luther and in modern Lutheranism. These three approaches are presented here somewhat simplistically and I plan to devote most of our attention to Calvin, who is not only the closest to our tradition, but more importantly, he is the closest to the biblical pattern.

MARTIN LUTHER (1483–1546) AND THE GERMAN REFORMATION

We owe a great debt to Martin Luther, through whom God restored the precious truth of justification by faith alone. Nevertheless, Luther was cautious in changing the worship of the church. This struck me some years ago when I spent a year in Germany—the Lutheran church that I attended had a crucifix. Luther had no

---

2 Robert Godfrey, in "Reforming the Church's Singing," writes, "Zwingli believed that music was too powerful and too emotional to be used in Christian worship. Under the strong influence of Platonic philosophy, he argued that music would too easily move people away from focusing on the Word and its meaning for them. As a result, in Zurich singing was eliminated from worship in Zwingli's day. No musical instruments, no choirs and no congregational singing were permitted. In the place of singing, Zwingli had the congregation recite Scriptural passages antiphonally." Resource Center, Westminster Seminary California, April 2, 2012, https://www.wscal.edu/resource-center/reforming-the-churchs-singing.

fundamental objection to crucifixes. In fact, some of Luther's colleagues became impatient because Luther was slow to reform the liturgy of the church. Luther preferred to teach the people so that they would reform the worship in their own time and at their own pace. Luther therefore removed references to sacrifice from the liturgy of the mass; he restored the preaching of God's word to a central place; he conducted worship in the German language; and he gave both elements (the bread and the wine) to the worshiper. Philip Schaff, the church historian, writes:

> Luther began to reform public worship in 1523, but with caution, and in opposition to the radicalism of Karlstadt, who during the former's absence on the Wartburg had tumultuously abolished the mass, and destroyed the altars and pictures…He tried to save the truly Christian elements in the old order, and to reproduce them in the vernacular language for the benefit of the people…

Luther regarded ceremonies, the use of clerical robes, candles on the altar, the attitude of the minister in prayer, as matters of indifference which may be retained or abolished. In the revision of the baptismal service, 1526, he abolished the use of salt, spittle, and oil, but retained the exorcism in an abridged form.[3] Not only did he restore worship in the language of the people, but Luther also reformed the church's singing. Like Calvin, he emphasized the importance of congregational singing in praise to God. Schaff writes:

> To Luther belongs the extraordinary merit of having given the German people in their own tongue, and in a form eclipsing and displacing all former versions, the Bible, the

---

3   Schaff, *History of the Christian Church*, 7:486, 489.

catechism, and the hymn-book, so that God might speak directly to them in His word, and that they might directly speak to Him in their songs. He was a musician also, and composed tunes to some of his hymns. He is the Ambrose of German church poetry and church music. He wrote thirty-seven hymns.[4]

This was revolutionary in an age when the only singing was the "chanting of priests and choirs."[5] Probably the best known of Luther's hymns is *"Ein' feste Burg ist unser Gott"* ("A Mighty Fortress Is Our God") based on Psalm 46. While we would disagree with Luther's use of hymns, we appreciate his restoration of music to the people of God. Luther understood that God's people must sing, while he was less clear on what they should sing.

Luther and his colleague Andreas Karlstadt (1486–1541) disagreed sharply on the issue of liturgical reform. Karlstadt wanted to force a reformation of the liturgy against the religious scruples of the people and the magistrates. Luther chided him and his followers for their haste and lack of love. Historian Carlos M. Eire writes in his *War Against the Idols:*

> According to him [Karlstadt], it was a Christian's duty to effect the removal of images from his community, even against opposition, because it was a divine command to abolish such pollution. The opinion of the magistracy or of one's fellow citizens should not be taken into account, since legal restrictions placed on iconoclasm are like the crying of a child who does not know that a harmful object is being taken away from him.[6]

---

4   Ibid., 7:502.
5   Ibid., 7:501.
6   Carlos M. N. Eire, *War Against the Idols: The Reformation of Worship from Erasmus to Calvin* (New York, NY: Cambridge University Press, 1986), 65.

About Karlstadt's radical, and even violent, iconoclasm (the practice of removing, and even destroying or breaking, images), Luther lamented in 1525, "Doctor Andreas Karlstadt has deserted us, and on top of that has become our worst enemy."[7] It is not easy to ascertain the precise reasons for Luther's opposition to Karlstadt. Certainly, Luther did not agree with the violent manner in which Karlstadt and the common people acted, but there is more to it than a desire for decency and order and an opposition to rebellion. Eire explains:

> Luther says that the prohibition of images, like the Sabbath regulations and other ceremonies of Judaism, is not binding for Christians. The reference to images in the first commandment is interpreted by Luther as strictly a temporal law that has been abrogated by the New Covenant...Against Karlstadt's call for the removal of images from the Churches, Luther argues that it is more effective to first "tear them out of the heart through God's word," for when they are no longer in the heart, "they can do no harm when seen with the eyes."[8]

Other scholars agree that Luther did not have a principled objection to what other reformers condemned as idolatry. Horton Davies, in his *The Worship of the English Puritans*, contrasts the liturgical positions of Luther and Calvin:

> Luther's conception of the Bible was that it contained the articles of belief necessary for salvation, but that in matters of worship and church government the Bible is not to

---

7   Ibid.
8   Ibid., 70.

be treated as a new Leviticus. Calvin…regarded the Bible as authoritative in doctrine, *government and worship…*

The real difference between the Lutheran and Calvinist reforms in worship may be summed up as follows: Luther will have what is not specifically condemned by the Scriptures; whilst Calvin will have only what is ordained by God in the Scriptures. That is their fundamental disagreement.

If the Scriptures were to Luther "the cradle of Christ," they were to Calvin the declared will of God for every aspect of human life. If Luther deprecated the use of the scriptures as a liturgical directory on the score of its being relegated to the position of a "nova lex," a new Leviticus, Calvin asserted that the human ordering of the worship of God was mere presumptuousness, since God had already laid down how he was to be worshipped.[9]

The English reformers adopted Martin Luther's more cautious and conservative approach, which means that they preferred to conserve or preserve more of the medieval liturgy than did the other reformers, especially Calvin. Thomas Cranmer (1489–1556), for example, authored the *Book of Common Prayer*, which contained a new liturgy for the English people. Although it went through a number of revisions, for many Protestants the *Book of Common Prayer* did not go far enough—the Puritans viewed it as too popish, and they desired a purge of all "popish ceremonies" (such as clerical vestments, the practice of kneeling at the Lord's supper, the sign of the cross, and the use of the ring in weddings) from the worship of the Anglican church. Luther would have counseled patience with such things. He would have viewed them as indifferent things.

---

9   Horton Davies, *The Worship of the English Puritans* (Morgan, PA: Soli Deo Gloria Publications, 1997), 3, 16, 49 (emphasis added).

Many of the Puritans, dissatisfied with the worship in the Anglican church, became Nonconformists in England, suffering persecution from the Anglicans. Others traveled to the New World, especially New England in the United States, where they were free to worship God according to their conscience.

ULRICH ZWINGLI (1484–1531) AND THE SWISS REFORMATION

If Luther's approach to the reformation of worship was one of caution, the Swiss took a more iconoclastic approach. As noted earlier, iconoclasm is the practice of smashing images, often in a violent, disorganized, and even frenzied manner. Swiss iconoclasm was, however, in contrast to the radicalism of Karlstadt, and in the words of church historian Philip Schaff, "radical, but orderly."[10] The reformers, such as Ulrich Zwingli, preached against idolatry, with the result that the civil magistrates ordered the removal of images with the cooperation of the people. Carlos Eire traces the progress of iconoclasm across Europe at the time of the Reformation. His description of the removal of images in Zurich in June 1524 is representative:

A committee of twelve was appointed and a number of craftsmen were assigned to execute the removal of the images, and this order was swiftly carried out. The city architect and the three people's priests (Zwingli, Jud, and Engelhard) served as overseers to the project. This committee entered each Zurich church as a body, beginning on 20 June, and proceeded to remove all the images efficiently and without violence. At the end of two weeks every church had been cleared of statues, paintings,

---

10 Schaff, *History*, 8:58.

murals, altar decorations, votive lamps and carved choir stalls. The walls of each church were also whitewashed. Without images and without the Mass, the preaching of the Word and the fulfillment of the Word were no longer at odds in Zurich. The physical presence of the old cultus had been removed after much prodding on the part of the people, and the Reformed church was now a reality. The final act of iconoclasm had been legal and peaceful, but it had not taken place without previous violence and disobedience leading the way.[11]

Zwingli's approach was made possible because the Reformed held public disputations with the Roman Catholics in which the victor in the debate determined the religion of the region or Swiss canton. Across Switzerland, the Reformed easily vanquished their theological opponents. Therefore, the Swiss reformers enjoyed the support of the magistrate in their liturgical reforms, which was not always the case in other parts of Europe.

JOHN CALVIN (1509–64) AND THE REFORMATION IN STRASBOURG AND GENEVA

John Calvin developed the great principle of Reformed liturgy: the regulative principle of worship. According to that principle, we may worship God no otherwise than he has commanded in his word. In other words, God—not man—determines how God shall be worshiped. It is not enough that a certain practice is not forbidden, but we must find a clear warrant for it in the word of God. Only what is commanded may be included in the worship of the Almighty. Calvin in Geneva, John Knox in Scotland, and the Puritans in England insisted upon this point. There may have

---

11 Eire, *War Against the Idols*, 82–83.

been some disagreement on how the principle was applied, but the principle itself was clear. That principle is enshrined in the Heidelberg Catechism (1563):

> What doth God require in the second commandment? That we in no wise make any image of God, *nor worship him in any other way than he has commanded in his Word.*[12]

For Calvin, whose chief aim in life and death was to glorify God, the worship of God was of supreme importance. In fact, Calvin viewed the worship of God as more important than the salvation of souls. Therefore, it is no surprise that he exerted a tremendous amount of effort to restore the public worship of God to biblical purity. In his "The Necessity of Reforming the Church" (1543), Calvin states the importance of this most emphatically:

> If it be inquired, then, by what things chiefly the Christian religion has a standing existence amongst us, and maintains its truth, it will be found that the following two not only occupy the principal place, but comprehend under them all the other parts, and consequently the whole substance of Christianity, viz. *a knowledge, first, of the mode in which God is duly worshipped;* and, *secondly,* of the source from which salvation is to be obtained. When these are kept out of view, though we may glory in the name of Christians, our profession is empty and vain.[13]

No doubt, we would agree that salvation and worship are the chief parts of Christianity. But would we agree with Calvin's *order*?

---

12 Heidelberg Catechism Q&A 96, in Schaff, *Creeds of Christendom*, 3:343 (emphasis added).

13 John Calvin, "The Necessity of Reforming the Church," in *Tracts and Treatises on the Reformation of the Church*, trans. Henry Beveridge, vol. 1 (Grand Rapids, MI: Wm. B. Eerdmans Publishing Company, 1958), 126 (emphasis added).

Would we put the worship of God *first*? Would we put the worship of God first *before salvation*? Would we become impatient and say, "Calvin, surely when we have finished our evangelism, then we will seek to reform the worship of the church. Worship is surely a secondary issue"? Calvin might well rebuke us, as he did the Roman Catholic Cardinal Sadolet in his famous letter of 1539, "It is not very sound theology to confine a man's thoughts so much to himself, and not to set before him, as the prime motive of his existence, zeal to illustrate the glory of God."[14] In this emphasis, Calvin reflects the teaching of holy scripture: "This people have I formed for myself; they shall shew forth my praise" (Isa. 43:21). "That ye should shew forth the praises of him who hath called you out of darkness into his marvellous light" (1 Pet. 2:9).

Calvin understood how difficult it was to wean man off the perverse notion that he may worship God as he pleases. Therefore, he repeatedly inculcates the point throughout his writings: God alone determines how he shall be worshiped, while all worship invented by man is an abomination to the Almighty. In his "The Necessity of Reforming the Church" Calvin drives this principle home to the reader:

> I know how difficult it is to persuade the world that *God disapproves of all modes of worship not expressly sanctioned by His Word.* The opposite persuasion which cleaves to them, being seated, as it were, in their very bones and marrow, is, that whatever they do has in itself a sufficient sanction, provided it exhibits some kind of zeal for the honour of God. But since God not only regards as fruitless, but also plainly abominates, whatever we undertake

---

14 John Calvin, "Reply by John Calvin to Letter by Cardinal Sadolet to the Senate and People of Geneva," in ibid., 33.

from zeal to His worship, if at variance with His command, what do we gain by a contrary course?[15]

A little later he writes:

Having observed that the word of God is the test which discriminates between his true worship and that which is false and vitiated, we thence readily infer that the whole form of divine worship in general use in the present day is nothing but mere corruption. For men pay no regard to what God has commanded, or to what he approves, in order that they may serve him in a becoming manner, *but assume to themselves a license of devising modes of worship,* and afterwards obtruding them upon him as a substitute for obedience. If in what I say I seem to exaggerate, let an examination be made of all the acts by which the generality suppose that they worship God. *I dare scarcely except a tenth part as not the random offspring of their own brain. What more would we? God rejects, condemns, abominates all fictitious worship, and employs his Word as a bridle to keep us in unqualified obedience.* When shaking off this yoke, we wander after our own fictions, and offer to him a worship, the work of human rashness, how much soever it may delight ourselves, in his sight it is vain trifling, nay, vileness and pollution. The advocates of human traditions paint them in fair and gaudy colours; and Paul certainly admits that they carry with them a show of wisdom; but as God values obedience more than all sacrifices, *it ought to be sufficient for the rejection of any mode of worship, that it is not sanctioned by the command of God.*[16]

---

15 Calvin, "Necessity of Reforming the Church," in ibid., 128–29 (emphasis added).
16 Ibid., 132–33 (emphasis added).

While Calvin applies this to the Roman Catholic idolatry of his day, we may apply it to the human innovations popular in evangelical and Reformed churches today. God rejects and abominates fictitious worship (drama, liturgical dance, worship bands, puppet shows, and more), even when the worship is sincere and zealous! Calvin explains the principle to Cardinal Sadolet, reminding him of the supreme importance of worshiping God aright:

> I have also no difficulty in conceding to you, that there is nothing more perilous to our salvation than a preposterous and perverse worship of God. The primary rudiments, by which we are wont to train to piety those whom we wish to gain as disciples of Christ, are these; viz., *not to frame any new worship for themselves at random, and after their own pleasure, but to know that the only legitimate worship is that which he himself approved from the beginning.* For we maintain, what the sacred oracle declared, that obedience is more excellent than any sacrifice, (1 Sam. xv. 22.). *In short, we train them, by every means, to be contented with the one rule of worship which they have received from his mouth, and bid adieu to all fictitious worship.*[17]

Calvin included this principle in the catechetical instruction of the children of Geneva: "The only worship which he [God] approves is not that which it may please us to devise, but that which he hath of his own authority prescribed."[18]

In Calvin's treatment of the second commandment in the *Institutes*, he writes:

---

17 Calvin, "Reply to Sadolet," 34 (emphasis added).
18 John Calvin, "The Catechism of the Church of Geneva," in *Tracts and Letters*, ed. and trans. Henry Beveridge, vol. 2 (Edinburgh, Scotland: Banner of Truth, repr. 2009), 56.

To sum up, he [God] wholly calls us back, and withdraws us from petty carnal observances, which our stupid minds, crassly conceiving of God, are wont to devise. And then he makes us conform to his lawful worship, that is, a spiritual worship established by himself.[19]

While I could multiply quotes from the illustrious reformer, I have cited enough to demonstrate the point. Only that which is commanded by God may properly be a part of worship.

John Knox developed the same regulative principle of worship in Scotland. A few citations suffice to prove his agreement with Calvin on this matter:

All worshipping, honouring, or service *invented by the brain of man* in the religion of God, *without his express commandment*, is idolatry...

No honouring knows God, nor will [he] accept, *without it having the express commandment of his own word* to be done in all points...

Disobedience to God's voice is not only when a man does wickedly contrary to the precepts of God, but also when of good zeal, or good intent (as we commonly speak), man does anything to the honour or service of God *not commanded by the express word of God*, as in the matter plainly may be espied...

Nothing in his religion will he [God] accept without his own word; but *all that is added thereto does he abhor, and punishes the inventors and doers thereof*.[20]

---

19 Calvin, *Institutes*, 2.8.17, 1:383.
20 John Knox, "A Vindication of the Doctrine that the Sacrifice of the Mass is Idolatry," in *Selected Writings of John Knox: Public Epistles, Treatises, and Expositions to the Year 1559* (Dallas, TX: Presbyterian Heritage Publications, 1995), 23, 24, 25–26, 27 (emphasis added).

John Hart, writing in the *Calvin Theological Journal*, takes note of the general uniformity of worship between Reformed and Presbyterian churches in England, America, and the European continent, a uniformity grounded in a common principle.

> While granting liberty and flexibility in the order of worship, Presbyterians in England and America, and Reformed on the Continent, followed remarkably similar patterns and agreed upon the elements that should constitute public worship. Those elements *ordinarily* included prayer, psalm-singing, the reading and preaching of the word, and the sacraments. The uniformity of agreement in Europe, Britain, and America reflected theological principle, not the cultural preferences of white middle-class men. The leaders of Presbyterian and Reformed churches may have been Caucasian, bourgeois, and male, but they believed their services exhibited the proper way to please God, not a means of church growth.[21]

WORSHIP IN GENEVA IN CALVIN'S DAY

Having established the principle, we should examine how Calvin applied it in Geneva. First, Calvin, in common with all the reformers, restored the preaching of God's word to the center of divine worship. Gone were the "old wives' fables, and fictions equally frivolous" prevalent in Roman Catholicism.[22] Instead, the word of God was preached! Calvin was nothing if not a preacher.

We can scarcely appreciate what a radical change this was. Now the people of God, for the first time, heard in their own language the exposition of the scriptures. Perhaps it is akin to the

---

21 D. G. Hart, "It May Be Refreshing, But Is It Reformed?" *Calvin Theological Journal* 32, no. 2 (November 1997): 408; Hart's italics.

22 Calvin, "Necessity of Reforming the Church," in *Tracts and Treatises*, 146.

amazement of the multitude of Jewish pilgrims at Pentecost: "We do hear them speak *in our tongues* the wonderful works of God" (Acts 2:11, emphasis added). We must not take for granted the precious gift of the pure preaching of God's word among us, for when a church begins to drift from the truth, the centrality of preaching is one of the first elements of worship to be lost. Indeed, it is vain to sing the psalms if the gospel of God's grace is not preached.

In his appeal to the emperor, Charles V, Calvin defends the practice of expository preaching.

> Our reformers have done no small service to the Church, in stirring up the world as from the deep darkness of ignorance, to read the Scriptures, in laboring diligently to make them better understood, and in happily throwing light on certain points of doctrine of the highest practical importance.[23]

English reformer and martyr Hugh Latimer (1487–1555), in his famous "Sermon on the Plough" (1548), has this to say about preaching:

> Where the devil is resident and hath his plough going, there away with books, and up with candles; away with Bibles, and up with beads; away with the light of the Gospel, and up with the light of candles, yea, at noon-days. Where the devil is resident, that he may prevail, up with all superstition and idolatry: censing, painting of images, candles, palms, ashes, holy water, and new service of men's inventing, as though man could invent a better way to honour God with than God Himself hath appointed.

---

23 Ibid.

Down with Christ's cross, up with purgatory pickpurse…
Away with clothing the naked, the poor and impotent; up
with decking of images, and gay garnishing of stocks and
stones: up with man's traditions and his laws, down with
God's traditions and His most holy Word.[24]

Philip Schaff, in his analysis of the reformers in general, takes
note of "the prominence given to the sermon, or the exposition
and application of the word of God, [which] became the chief part
of divine service, and as regards importance took the place of the
mass."[25]

T. H. L. Parker, a biographer of the great reformer, draws a
beautiful portrait of Calvin the preacher:

There is no threshing himself into a fever of impatience
or frustration, no holier-than-thou rebuking of the people, no begging them in terms of hyperbole to give some
physical sign that the message has been accepted. It is
simply one man, conscious of his sins, aware how little
progress he makes and how hard it is to be a doer of the
Word, sympathetically passing on to his people (whom he
knows to have the same sort of problems as himself) what
God has said to them and to him.[26]

Second, Calvin restored the practice of congregational singing to the church in Geneva, a practice that he had learned from
Martin Bucer (1491–1551) in Strasbourg. As early as 1536, Calvin
insisted on this:

---

24 Philip E. Hughes, *Theology of the English Reformers* (Grand Rapids, MI: William
   B. Eerdmans Publishing Company, 1965), 129.
25 Schaff, *History*, 7:490.
26 T. H. L. Parker, *Calvin's Preaching* (Edinburgh, Scotland: T&T Clark, 1992), 119.

Worship should include the congregational singing of psalms, so as to give fervour and ardour to the prayers which otherwise are apt to be dead and cold. Since, however, neither tunes nor words are known to the congregation, many of whom are probably illiterate, there shall be a children's choir which shall sing clearly. The people for their part shall listen "with all attention" and gradually pick up the words and music.[27]

Calvin enlisted the children of the church, who most easily learn the lyrics and tunes of songs, to help the adults to sing the praises of God in the public assemblies. Writing in the *Calvin Theological Journal*, John D. Witvliet explains:

In the Reformation era, the whole congregation sang—men, women, and children together—an innovation in an era when women's voices could otherwise be heard in worship only in a convent. The children, for their part, were the leaders of the song. In the 1537 Articles, Calvin had instructed:

"This manner of proceeding seemed especially good to us, that children, who beforehand have practiced some modest church song, sing in a loud distinct voice, the people listening with all attention and following heartily what is sung with the mouth, till all become accustomed to sing communally."[28]

The reason for the prevalence of congregational singing in Calvin's Geneva is simple, according to Parker.

---

27 T. H. L. Parker, *John Calvin: A Full-Scale Life of the Controversial Reformation Leader and Influential Theologian* (Tring, Herts., England: Lion Publishing plc., 1975), 76.

28 John D. Witvliet, "The Spirituality of the Psalter: Metrical Psalms in Liturgy and Life in Calvin's Geneva," *Calvin Theological Journal* 32, no. 2 (November 1997): 280.

The reason is not far to seek. To put it with the utmost simplicity: the church is the place where the gospel is preached; gospel is good news; good news makes people happy; happy people sing. But then, too, unhappy people may sing to cheer themselves up—"Art thou weary? Music will charm thee."[29]

This contradicts the caricature of Calvin and Calvinists as sour, joyless Puritans. Calvin was a man who knew the joy of salvation, and he preached to a people who knew the joy of salvation. Joyous believers love to sing, and Calvin made sure that they sang the best material that he could find—the God-breathed psalms of David, the very odes of the Holy Spirit!

He wanted the people to sing joyously. There is no reason for God's redeemed saints to sing as if they were at a funeral! Calvin writes in the preface to the Genevan Psalter (1562):

> Now what Saint Augustine says is true, that no one is able to sing things worthy of God unless he has received them from him. Wherefore, when we have looked thoroughly everywhere and searched high and low, we shall find no better songs nor more appropriate for the purpose than the Psalms of David, which the Holy Spirit made and spoke through him. And furthermore, when we sing them, we are certain that God puts the words in our mouths, as if he himself were singing in us to exalt his glory.[30]

Skilled musicians, such as Clement Marot (1496–1544) and Louis Bourgeois (c. 1510–59), were employed in the task of producing a psalter from which the Genevan congregation could

---

29 Parker, *John Calvin*, 104.
30 "Preface to the Psalter," Eclectic Ethereal Encyclopedia, can be accessed at https://www.ccel.org/ccel/ccel/eee/files/calvinps.htm.

sing. Clearly, Calvin desired only the best musical material to be used in the worship of the Almighty. In his "The Necessity of Reforming the Church," Calvin describes the worship in Geneva: "in our churches, all pray in common in the popular tongue, and males and females indiscriminately sing the Psalms."[31] Men, women, young people, and children singing the psalms together in public worship is a thoroughly Calvinistic and Reformed practice. Hymn singing, special numbers, or choirs is not.

Hughes Oliphant Old remarks,

> The Reformers wanted the whole congregation to sing the praises of the church. They wanted the people to sing in their own language and in music simple enough for the people to learn. This meant, quite practically speaking, the production of a wholly new church music.[32]

Notice that Calvin did not set out to write new songs, what the modern world calls "hymns." Calvin had no place for hymns; he insisted on the singing of the psalms. If Calvin had wanted to promote the singing of hymns, he could have enlisted the help of musicians and hymn writers. Instead, he enlisted their help to translate from the Hebrew and then put to song the psalms of David, with the result that by the end of Calvin's life the whole Psalter was sung in the public worship of the churches in Geneva. In fact, the only two songs that the churches in Geneva sang *apart from the psalms* were the song of Simeon and the ten commandments, both inspired writings from the holy scriptures.

Writing in the *Calvin Theological Journal*, John D. Witvliet offers some interesting insights:

---

31 Calvin, "Necessity of Reforming the Church," in *Tracts and Treatises*, 159.
32 Hughes Oliphant Old, *Worship: Reformed according to Scripture* (Louisville, KY: Westminster John Knox Press, 2002), 42.

The importance of the psalter is also underscored by the high priority it had with the Genevan reformers. *The call for sung psalmody in worship was one of Calvin's first acts of liturgical reform and one to which he was dedicated throughout his life.* Calvin first heard psalm singing during his first visit to Strasbourg, where Protestant congregations had, by the mid-1530s, a decade of experience in singing the psalms in worship. Already in the first paragraph of his 1537 *Articles for Church Organization*, Calvin called for singing psalms "for the edification of the church." Then, in 1539, Calvin released his first psalter, the *Aulcuns pseaulmes et cantiques mys en chant*, for his exile congregation in Strasbourg. It was a collection of twenty-two texts by Clement Marot and Calvin himself that were set to tunes drawn primarily from the earlier German psalters…Several editions of the evolving psalter were printed in Geneva during the next two decades, eventually incorporating the tunes of Louis Bourgeois, who came to Geneva in 1542 as a music educator, and later, the metrical translations of Theodore Beza, who finished where Marot had left off prior to his departure from Geneva. Finally, the complete Genevan Psalter was issued in 1562, a volume with 152 texts—each psalm, the Ten Commandments, and the Song of Simeon—set to 125 different tunes.[33]

A little later he notes that:

What Calvin did not allow was the accompaniment of this song by instruments of any kind. For Calvin, instrumental music in worship properly belonged only to the

---

33 Witvliet, "Spirituality of the Psalter," 275–76 (emphasis added).

Old Testament dispensation. As Calvin advised, when the biblical writers spoke of musical instruments, it "was not as if this were in itself necessary." Rather, instrumental music "was useful as an elementary aid to the people of God in these ancient times," an aid that was no longer necessary after Christ.[34]

The process of producing a psalter was not without controversy, however. Louis Bourgeois, one of the greatest musicians of his day and the composer of the celebrated tune Old One Hundredth, learned how passionate the people can be about the songs and tunes to which they have been accustomed:

> [He] fell foul of local musical authorities and was sent to prison on December 3, 1551 for changing the tunes for some well-known psalms "without a license." He was released on the personal intervention of John Calvin, but the controversy continued. Those who had already learned the tunes had no desire to learn new versions, and the town council ordered the burning of Bourgeois's instructions to the singers, claiming they were confusing. Shortly after this incident, Bourgeois left Geneva never to return.[35]

---

34 Ibid., 281.

35 "Louis Bourgeois (composer)", *Wikipedia*, last modified September 13, 2017, https://en.wikipedia.org/wiki/Louis_Bourgeois_(composer). Another writer explains, "At all events on 3 December 1551 Bourgeois was imprisoned for having, without a license, 'changed the tunes of some printed psalms', an action troubling those who had learnt the old tunes that had already been printed. He was released the following day after Calvin's personal intercession, but the controversy continued: the council complained further that the faithful were disorientated by the new melodies, and ordered Crespin to burn the prefatory epistle to the reader in which Bourgeois claimed that not to sing was commination" ("Louise Bourgeois, (Composer)," *Bach Cantatas Website*, last updated September 2005, http://www.bach-cantatas.com/Lib/Bourgeois-Louis.htm). The *Encyclopedia Britannica* states, "Bourgeois was made a citizen of Geneva in 1547. In 1551 he was imprisoned for a day for tampering with the accepted

For those critics of the psalms we should note that Reformed psalm singing, although reverent, as becomes the worship of God, was not, and should never be, cold and boring. Calvin writes, "Certainly as things are, the prayers of the faithful are so cold, that we ought to be ashamed and dismayed. The psalms can incite us to lift up our hearts to God and move us to an ardour in invoking and exalting with praises the glory of his Name."[36] In another place, he writes, "Unquestionably we do exhort men to worship God *neither in a frigid nor a careless manner*."[37] Parker recounts the reaction of a French-speaking refugee from the Lowlands to the singing of the people in Strasbourg:

> Everyone sings, men and women, and *it is a lovely sight.* Each has a music book in his hand…For five or six days at the beginning as I looked on this little company of exiles, *I wept*, not for sadness but *for joy to hear them all singing so heartily*, and as they sang giving thanks to God that he had led them to a place where his name is glorified. *No one could imagine what joy there is* in singing the praises and wonders of the Lord in the mother tongue as they are sung here.[38]

So popular were the psalms that the people of God sang them in the fields and in the shops as they did their work. Do our hearts express such strong feelings when we sing God's praises from the psalms of David today?

Psalm tunes without authorization, but Calvin secured his release, and eventually Bourgeois' alterations were approved" ("Loys Bourgeois," *Encyclopedia Britannica*, https://www.britannica.com/biography/Loys-Bourgeois). For further study, read http://psalmsmusic.wursten.be/bourgeois-loys.html.

36 Witvliet, "Spirituality of the Psalter," 282.

37 Calvin, "Necessity of Reforming the Church," in *Tracts and Treatises*, 1:146 (emphasis added).

38 Parker, *John Calvin*, 83 (emphasis added).

Whereas Roman Catholic sensibilities preferred to draw a clear line between liturgy and secular life, the Calvinists freely sang these texts and tunes in their homes and fields. The same impulse that led the Reformers to question medieval monasticism, the same influence that drove Calvin to extend the influence of the Gospel to every nook and cranny of Genevan life was mirrored in the very way these metrical psalms were used.[39]

Indeed, a typical worship service in Geneva in Calvin's day was, as to its elements, remarkably similar to one of our worship services today. Most of us would feel "right at home" in such a service, if we could understand late medieval French, of course. A typical service included the votum ("Our help is in the name of the Lord who made heaven and earth"), prayers (a mixture of form prayers and extemporaneous prayers), the singing of psalms, (the singing of) the law, the (singing of the) Apostles' Creed, the confession of sin and the pronouncement of absolution, the collection of alms for the poor, the reading of scripture, the preaching of the word, and a closing benediction.[40] Calvin also advocated the frequent partaking of the Lord's supper, which, when celebrated, was administered with a very simple service after the sermon. Apart from the singing of the law and the creed and the service of absolution, Calvin's service is almost identical to our services today. We ought not be ashamed or embarrassed at that, but rejoice in it. God has preserved pure worship among us!

---

39 Witvliet, "Spirituality of the Psalter," 297.
40 See Hart, "It May Be Refreshing, But Is It Reformed?" 407.

CONCLUSION

Finally, did the Reformation tear down the three barriers mentioned at the beginning of the chapter? Indeed, it did! The Reformation restored right worship to God's people. Instead of worshiping idols, the people returned to the pure worship of God; instead of enduring an incomprehensible and complicated liturgy in Latin, the people worshiped God with understanding in their own language; and instead of being spectators, the people actively participated in the worship, especially in congregational singing and the attentive hearing of God's word, because to them had been restored the rights and privileges of the office of believer.

We close with some practical applications. As sons and daughters of the Protestant Reformation, we want to follow in the footsteps of our spiritual forefathers. What do we learn from them regarding the right worship of God?

First, we learn jealously to guard the worship of God from innovation. Is there a push to bring new elements into the worship, to make the worship seeker sensitive, to add more entertainment to the worship, to make the worship appeal to the young people, or to make the worship "modern"? We must resist such pressure, for worship is not about us; it concerns the glory of God. Incidentally, drama, liturgical dance, choirs, special numbers, and uninspired hymns are *not* modern, but they are medieval. The reformers were familiar with these things, but they rejected them. They did so deliberately because God does not explicitly command them in his word. Therefore, they have no place in the worship of the church.

Second, we learn that our worship should be joyous. We have a reason to sing praises to God, to listen attentively to the preaching of the gospel, and to give of our gifts. We have a reason to gather with our children before the face of our God in public worship.

We are God's redeemed children. Therefore, our worship, while reverent, should not be a funeral dirge but a joyous celebration of God's mercies. The restoration of right worship is a consequence of the recovery of the gospel of grace.

Third, we must resist any attempt to reconstruct the liturgical barriers erected by the Roman Catholic Church and torn down by the reformers. We must resist the reintroduction of priests, of idols and visual aids (the only visual aids permitted in public worship are the sacraments), of foreign language barriers (away with the unknown tongues of charismaticism!), and we must never allow liturgical innovators to make us idle spectators again. As prophets, priests, and kings, we have the right and privilege to worship God.

Instead, we say with the psalmist of old, "I was glad when they said unto me, Let us go into the house of the LORD" (Ps. 122:1). We will come, eager to worship our God, with our children; eager to hear what God has to say to us, his beloved people; and eager to respond to him with heartfelt, thankful praise and prayer as we call upon his name.

Chapter 5

THE REFORMATION'S RESPONSE TO THE RADICAL REFORMATION

Russell J. Dykstra

≋

> *Be ye therefore very courageous to keep and to do all that is*
> *written in the book of the law of Moses, that ye turn not aside*
> *therefrom to the right hand or to the left.*
>
> —JOSHUA 23:6

The Radical Reformation? What is that? Most Reformed and Presbyterian people have some knowledge of the great sixteenth-century Reformation. They recognize the names of the men God raised up to reform his church, men such as Luther, Calvin, Zwingli, and Knox. However, the topic of this chapter is an aspect of the Reformation of which many know relatively little.

The Radical Reformation was a movement consisting of people who were initially a part of the Reformation. They left the Romish church, rejecting the teachings and worship of Rome. Many of them became followers of Luther and, for a time, were active supporters of the Reformation. But for various reasons, they moved beyond Luther and the other reformers and began to take radical positions and maintain radical teachings.

This was an extremely varied group.[1] It consisted first of Anabaptists, a word that means baptized again. Anabaptists rejected infant baptism and therefore rebaptized adults who confessed their faith—hence the name. Spiritualists, men who claimed to receive special revelations from the Holy Spirit, were another part of the Radical Reformation. Still another part consisted of radical revolutionaries who tried to take over cities in the name of Christ and establish a new kingdom of Christ on the earth. Finally, under this broad umbrella were heretics of the worst kind, who denied every biblical truth that they could not prove rationally, even such foundational doctrines as the Trinity and the incarnation.

THE IMPORTANCE OF THE RADICAL REFORMATION

Reformed believers understand that God is in control of all men and events, also the entire Reformation. God determined that this aspect of the Reformation would surface. Even though these men did damage to the Reformation movement in places, in the end, they served the good of God's church. The radical movement forced the church to develop in doctrine and practice as she would not have developed without these radicals.

This is true from a number of perspectives, the first of which is doctrinal. The errors of the radicals forced the reformers to develop their doctrines more clearly and sharply over against these heresies. The reformers were standing between two bodies

---

1   The single most comprehensive work on the Radical Reformation is George Huntston Williams's book *The Radical Reformation*, ed. Charles G. Nauert (Philadelphia, PA: Westminster Press, 1962). Williams demonstrated that the Radical Reformation was much more diverse than the term Anabaptist could encompass, and he coined the name Radical Reformation. For a briefer but excellent historical overview, see Nick Needham, "Flowers for the Bees: The Radical Reformation," chap. 5 in *2000 years of Christ's Power, Volume 3, Renaissance and Reformation* (Scotland: Christian Focus Publications Ltd., 2016), 251–320.

of errors. On the one hand, the reformers rejected the pernicious errors of Rome—her idolatry, works-righteousness and Pelagianism, the hierarchy and authority of the pope, and her abuse of scripture, to name a few. The reformers rejected the entire sacerdotal system of the seven sacraments, especially the mass, and purgatory. On the other hand, the reformers had to stand firm against the false teachings of the Radical Reformation—their rejection of infant baptism, wrong ideas of the church and sacraments, their rejection of the authority of magistrates, as well as errors on the second coming of Christ and his kingdom, on the Holy Spirit, and more.

In his masterful reply to the Roman Catholic Cardinal Sadolet, Calvin specifically identified these two enemies of the Reformation:

> We are assailed by two sects, which seem to differ most widely from each other. For what similitude is there in appearance between the Pope and the Anabaptists? And yet, that you may see that Satan never transforms himself so cunningly, as not in some measure to betray himself, the principal weapon with which they both assail us is the same. For when they boast extravagantly of the Spirit, the tendency certainly is to sink and bury the word of God, that they may make room for their own falsehoods.[2]

The Radical Reformation's effect on the Reformation was important also from a historical perspective. As will be demonstrated, some of the radicals incited rebellion against the rulers in Europe in various places. These revolutions, which were associated with the Reformation, provided the Roman Catholic rulers with an excuse to persecute and kill the Reformed believers, for

---

2 John Calvin, "Reply to Cardinal Sadolet," in *Tracts and Treatises*, 1:36.

the radicals claimed that the biblical basis for a change in religion found in the Reformation was also justification for a social revolution. Some claimed that Luther's theology was the ground for insurrection against magistrates.

The opponents of the Reformation seized the opportunity to charge the reformers with the responsibility for revolution, and they condemned the entire Reformation as revolutionary. This charge would dog the Reformation all through its history. The Roman Catholic rulers could claim that they were only persecuting the Anabaptists. The reformers rejected the charge, but it was a difficult task to convince the rulers that they were different from the radicals.

The impact of the Radical Reformation, doctrinally and historically, demands that we examine how the true Reformation responded to it. We can divide the material into various sections. First, I will give a brief overview of the movement: its history and its doctrinal positions. The treatment of the Radical Reformation can hardly be exhaustive, for the movement was varied and its effects were felt in all the countries of Europe where the Reformation was found. In the examining the Reformation's response to the Radical Reformation, I will begin with Martin Luther's response to the radicals who stirred up trouble in the church in Wittenberg. Next, we will learn how John Calvin dealt with the radicals. Finally, we will set forth some lessons for today.

A BRIEF OVERVIEW:
HISTORY OF THE RADICAL REFORMATION

One of the first notable instances in which radicalism reared its head occurred in the birthplace of the Reformation, namely, Wittenberg, Germany. The radical spirit arose in Wittenberg at a time when Luther was in hiding. After the Diet of Worms in

April 1921, Emperor Charles V put Luther under the ban, which meant that he was condemned, and his life was in danger. Luther was "kidnapped" by supporters and brought for safekeeping to the Wartburg castle, where he lived for eleven months under the name Knight George.

During that extended absence of Luther, radicals took over the reformation in Wittenberg. The leader of this group was Andreas Bodenstein von Karlstadt. He was a friend of Luther, a man who had stood with Luther from the early days of the Reformation. He even engaged in public debates with the representatives of Rome. However, in Luther's absence, he began to promote radical measures.

Karlstadt started with the Lord's supper. Luther had not led the church in Wittenberg to adopt many changes in the liturgy that they had received from Rome. He was of the conviction that what was not forbidden by scripture might be allowed in the worship services. Although Luther rejected the doctrine of the mass—transubstantiation—and rejected the worship of the elements, he had done little to change the manner in which the Lord's supper was administered. The practice of the church included that the members confessed their sins to a priest (now the minister) before coming to take communion. During the service, each member came to the altar and kneeled, and the priest (now the minister) placed the wafer in the mouth of the member.

Karlstadt, rightly rejecting the evils of the Romish mass, was convinced that it was time to make more drastic changes. First, he rejected the need for confession of sin to a man before partaking of the Lord's supper. The believer, he preached, confesses his sins only to God, and therefore Karlstadt forbad the practice. Second, whereas in the past only the priest was allowed to partake of both elements—bread and wine—Karlstadt insisted that from now on all the communicants must partake of both elements. In addition, he pressured the people to take hold of the elements with their own hands in order to partake of them. After years and years of observing the Romish practices, some of the people were terrified that they were sinning by following these changes.

Karlstadt's manner of dealing with the people is evident from a sermon that he preached in Wittenberg on December 25, 1521, entitled, "Concerning the Reception of the Holy Sacrament."[3] In this sermon he faced the question, "How can one determine worthiness for the sacrament?" His answer: only from scripture, especially the New Testament. He warned the hearers that they could not make themselves worthy by prayer, fasting, confession, or penance. They must not fear sin, he assured them, for the sacrament is for sinners. They must not fear God's anger, for "God... reproaches no one for his wickedness."[4] The only concern must be unbelief—that makes one unworthy. Believe in Christ; believe his words and promises, he exhorted. "Consequently, fitness and worthiness depend on faith alone."[5] Without faith, he warned, "you must die and you are spiritually dead before you eat of the Lord's bread and wine—just as Aaron died because he did not believe the divine mouth."[6]

Karlstadt taught that Jesus' promise to the believer in the Lord's supper is that he would enjoy a harmless death and a joyful resurrection, and that "the sign of the bread produces nothing other than certainty and assurance of the aforesaid promise."[7] The people must not fear death, for believers have escaped the curse

---

3 Ronald J. Sider, ed., *Karlstadt's Battle with Luther: Documents in a Liberal-Radical Debate* (Philadelphia, PA: Fortress Press, 1978), 7–15.
4 Ibid., 8.
5 Ibid., 9.
6 Ibid., 9–10.
7 Ibid., 10.

of the law: "Christ makes me share in all his righteousness and fulfillment of the law."[8]

In the sermon, Karlstadt answered certain objections to his rejection of the need for confession of sins to a man. To those who would say, "I may not drink the cup without going to confession," he replied, "Christ said, 'Take it and drink.'" He reasoned, "If you obtain forgiveness of sins beforehand in confession, what then do you want to do with the sacrament?"[9] If you need forgiveness before you partake, he argued, then you have no faith in the words of Christ. "Seek forgiveness of sins in the gospel of the cup."[10] He was amazed that someone would believe a minister who declared one absolved of guilt, but did not believe the gospel of the cup.

Karlstadt next turned to the monasteries. Luther had openly condemned the evils in the Roman Catholic monasteries. Karlstadt followed up on Luther's strong language and emptied the monasteries and convents, turning out the monks and nuns who had taken vows of chastity for life and strongly encouraging them to marry.

Karlstadt saw more that needed reform. He loathed the idolatry of Rome and started destroying the pictures of the saints and the images of Jesus found in their churches. Rejecting the long-standing practice prescribed by the medieval church of refraining from eating meat on Fridays, Karlstadt began compelling people to eat meat on Friday.

Then Karlstadt received reinforcements from two "prophets" from Zwickau—Niklas Storch and Thomas Stubner. These men claimed to receive special messages from the Holy Spirit, and they supported Karlstadt's "reforms" in Wittenberg. Pressing the importance of the truth that every believer has the Spirit, they

---

8   Ibid., 11.
9   Ibid., 12–13.
10 Ibid., 13.

denigrated the value of Bible study. Under their influence some of the schools in Wittenberg were closed—for why should the children need to know how to read the Bible when they could receive direct guidance from the Spirit?

All these changes were carried out in the brief period of eleven months that Luther spent in Wartburg castle, and they forced him out of hiding. Later, we will examine Luther's response to these radical reforms upon his return to Wittenberg.

REBELLION AND REVOLUTION

The radical movement took a violent turn in what is known as the Peasants' Rebellion of 1525. To put this in context, it must be noted that the peasants were terribly oppressed in virtually all the countries of Europe. Generally, their masters cared little for them, whether they prospered or starved. Many uprisings had occurred in the past in different regions of Europe. Various documents were drawn up by the peasants in which they requested relief. One of them addressed the "honorable, wise, and favorable lords, friends, and dear neighbors" with this plea:

> In the recent past heavy burdens, much against God and all justice, have been imposed on the poor and common man in the cities and in the countryside by spiritual and worldly lords and authorities. But these [impositions] have not touched these lords in the slightest way. The result is that these burdens and grievances can no longer be borne or tolerated, unless the common man is willing to condemn himself and his progeny to a life of begging.[11]

---

11 "The Document of Articles of the Black Forest Peasants," in *The Radical Reformation*, ed. and trans. Michael G. Baylor (Cambridge: Cambridge University Press, 1991), 243–44.

In their "Twelve Articles of the Upper Swabian Peasants," some of the peasants requested the freedom to select their own preacher and to dismiss him if he misbehaved. They requested the right to hunt for food in open fields and to fish from the rivers, and to take wood for their use in those areas not legally owned, but only claimed, by the lords. They objected to their being considered the property of the lords (a remnant of the feudal system of the medieval age), as well as being forced to work for the lords without pay. They requested relief from being forced to pay crushing taxes both to earthly rulers and to the church rulers. They grounded their requests on specific passages of the Bible and concluded that "if one or more of the articles…is not in accordance with the word of God," they would retract the articles.[12]

Luther was himself from a peasant background. He had written and preached that the masters ought to treat the peasants with more kindness and the love of God. The peasants therefore had some reason to believe that Luther would support their cause.

The discontent of the peasants in Germany steadily grew to a fever pitch. One of the driving forces behind this rebellion was a radical named Thomas Müntzer. Müntzer was born into a well-to-do family in the region of Thüringen in 1488 or 1489. Norman Cohn indicates that Müntzer was "extraordinarily learned and intensely intellectual."[13] Müntzer was given a very good education. "Profoundly versed in the scriptures, he learned Greek and Hebrew, read patristic and scholastic theology and philosophy, immersed himself also in the writings of the German mystics." Cohn describes Müntzer as "a troubled soul, full of doubts about the truth of Christianity and even about the existence of God."[14]

---

12 Ibid., 231–38.
13 Norman Cohn, *The Pursuit of the Millennium* (New York, NY: Oxford University Press, 1970), 235.
14 Ibid.

Müntzer first forsook the church of Rome and joined with the cause of Luther, but he "abandoned Luther almost as soon as he had found him; and it was in ever fiercer opposition to Luther that he worked out and proclaimed his own doctrine."[15]

In 1520, Müntzer took up a ministry in the town of Zwickau. There he came into contact with a weaver named Niklas Storch (one of the two "prophets" who came to Wittenberg). Storch believed that the end of the ages was very near and that in that age God would communicate directly with the elect. He contended that he was one of those who had such direct communication with God. God's message was that the elect must rise up and extermi-nate all the ungodly in preparation for the coming of Christ. The elect are those who receive the Holy Spirit. Müntzer became an ardent preacher of the same doctrine, and he was certain that he could determine who were elect and who were not.

> According to Cohn, Müntzer claimed to have "perfect insight into the divine will" and believed he was "incon-testably qualified to discharge the divinely appointed eschatological mission."[16] His radical preaching caused an uprising in Zwickau in April 1521. When the revolt was put down, he was forced to leave. He was undaunted. Traveling through Bohemia, he preached (in a sermon on the wheat and the tares) that "harvest-time is here, so God himself has hired me for his harvest. I have sharpened my scythe, for my thoughts are more strongly fixed on the truth, and my lips, hands, skin, hair, soul, body, life curse the unbelievers."[17]

---

15 Ibid.
16 Ibid., 236–37.
17 Ibid., 237.

Müntzer's language became increasingly strident in calls for the elect to kill all the ungodly. In a letter sent to his followers he urged them:

> Now go at them, and at them, and at them! It is time. The scoundrels are as dispirited as dogs…It is very, very necessary, beyond measure necessary…Take no notice of the lamentation of the godless! They will beg you in such a friendly way, and whine and cry like children. Don't be moved to pity…Stir up in villages and towns.[18]

He also took it upon himself to address rulers, whether in person or by threatening letters, as in this missive to a certain Count Earnest of Mansfeld:

> Say, you wretched, shabby bag of worms, who made you a prince over the people whom God has purchased with his precious blood?…By God's mighty power you are delivered up to destruction. If you do not humble yourself before the lowly, you will be saddled with everlasting infamy in the eyes of all Christendom and will become the Devil's martyr.[19]

Müntzer and other self-proclaimed preachers maintained that the peasants were free. If Luther could proclaim that the pope had no authority to rule the soul, surely the people were free to serve God and could throw off the oppression of the wicked rulers. Thus encouraged, the peasants revolted, raising up ragtag armies of ill-trained and poorly equipped men.

If they expected to have Martin Luther's support of their uprisings, the peasants were to be sorely disappointed. In typically clear

---

18 Ibid., 247.
19 Ibid., 249.

and forceful language, Luther condemned the peasants' uprising, publishing in 1525 the treatise "Against the Robbing and Murdering Hordes of Peasants." In it, Luther encouraged the rulers to kill the rebels, which they did, including Thomas Müntzer.

One significant effect of this uprising was that Luther never again fully trusted the peasants. That in turn had a significant impact on the churches that Luther founded. When it came time to organize church government, Luther advocated putting the rule of the church into the hands of the Christian rulers, a form of church government known as Erastian.

It should be noted that Thomas Müntzer never explicitly identified with the Anabaptist movement. At the same time, he does represent the extreme radicals who left the church of Rome and associated with the Reformation in one way or another. That form of radicalism did not end with the squelching of the peasants' revolts in the 1520s. Less than ten years later an even more notable uprising arose—the Münster Rebellion, 1534–35.

Followers of Müntzer continued promoting the notion that the end of the world was near. Based on the teaching that the pope is the antichrist and the conviction that the world surely was ripe for the second coming of Christ, they predicted that Christ would come at any time and establish the kingdom of righteousness. Hans Hut, a well-known Anabaptist of that day, predicted the imminent return of Christ and insisted that it was necessary to gather 144,000 saints. His followers (many of them Dutch) took matters into their own hands. Jan Matthijs set up twelve apostles and declared himself to be Enoch and another man (Melchior Hoffmann) to be Elijah, claiming they two were the two witnesses foretold in Revelation 11.

In 1534 the Anabaptist radicals—led by Jan Matthijs and Jan Bockelson (usually known simply as Jan of Leyden)—took over the city of Münster in Germany and declared it the New Jerusalem. Most of the Lutherans and Roman Catholics left the city, but those who remained were required to be rebaptized. The leaders, through the seven deacons, took the wealth and goods of the rich and distributed it to the poor. Eventually they outlawed private ownership and instituted a community of goods. As Jan of Leyden later expressed it, "All things were to be in common, there was to be no private property and nobody was to do any more work, but simply trust in God."[20] Jan of Leyden claimed to receive special revelations. He declared himself the King of Righteousness, instituted polygamy, and took several wives to himself. Anyone who opposed his rule or his laws was executed.

The response to this radical takeover was that all the area rulers, both Roman Catholic and Protestant, joined their armies and crushed the rebellion. The leaders who survived the fighting were captured and tortured without mercy until they died.

This rebellion would have a profound effect on the subsequent history of the Reformation. As noted earlier, the most significant consequence was that this event would lead the Romish church and rulers to brand the Reformation as revolutionary, in spite of the fact that both Protestant and Roman Catholic rulers put down the rebellion. The reformers constantly repudiated this charge and sought to distinguish themselves from these radicals. This effort is evident, for example, in the Belgic Confession, particularly in article 36 "On Magistrates," which includes this disavowal:

> Wherefore we detest the error of the Anabaptists and other seditious people, and in general all those who reject the higher powers and magistrates, and would subvert justice, introduce community of goods, and confound

---

20 Ibid., 265–66.

that decency and good order, which God hath established among men.[21]

THE ANABAPTISTS

In all the major Reformation cities, including Zurich, Strasbourg, and Geneva, diverse, though generally less revolutionary, groups of radicals appeared. These groups became known as Anabaptists. Because the reformers would be forced to deal with their theology, it is important to know something of their teaching.

A major concern of these groups was the purity of the church. This is related to their rejection of infant baptism. Before the Reformation, the church baptized all the children of a given city if possible, thus making them members of the church and, by this means, bringing them under the control of Rome. The theology of Rome supported this, since Rome taught that baptism washed away the original sin of Adam for every baptized person. Rome even insisted that a baby without baptism could not enter heaven. Understandably, virtually all parents in a given locale would bring their children for baptism. Many of these baptized members were, of course, not believers, and as they grew up their lives reflected their unbelief in godless living, while yet being officially members of the church.

The Reformation church tried to be more selective—not baptizing all children in the city, and yet baptizing almost every baby that parents brought. The result was a situation in which many members of society were baptized members of the church of the Reformation but lived ungodly lives.

Some members of the Reformation churches became convinced that the flaw in the system was infant baptism. They began

---

21 Belgic Confession 36, in Schaff, *Creeds of Christendom*, 3:433.

teaching that only believers ought to be baptized. They required a confession of faith before allowing baptism. These people began rebaptizing adults (hence the name "Anabaptists"), and they refused to bring their children for baptism, insisting that the New Testament scriptures recorded no baptism of infants. They sought a pure church, a church consisting only of true believers, who lived God-fearing lives.

Their intense quest for purity of life led them into significant errors in the doctrines of man and salvation. Most Anabaptists denied justification by faith alone. They viewed it as an excuse for careless living. Many also denied total depravity and insisted that fallen man had freedom of the will, able to choose to do good and to believe. Some also taught perfectionism, the notion that one could live without sin if he would but strive hard enough.

The Anabaptists' faulty theology respecting man's depravity led to unorthodox teaching on the human nature of Christ. Desiring to find a theological justification for the sinlessness of Christ, they came to the conclusion that Jesus' human nature was not derived from Mary. Rather, they taught that his human nature was a specially created nature that only passed through Mary's womb. Both the Heidelberg Catechism and the Belgic Confession are at pains to reject this error of the Anabaptists, the latter creed by name.[22]

A second concern of the Anabaptists was the government's

---

22 The Belgic Confession article 18, "Of the Incarnation of Jesus Christ," states, "Therefore we confess (in opposition to the heresy of the Anabaptists, who deny that Christ assumed human flesh of his mother) that Christ is become *a partaker of the flesh and blood of the children;* that he is a *fruit of the loins of David* after the flesh; *made of the seed of David according to the flesh;* a fruit of the womb of the Virgin Mary, *made of a woman*" (Schaff, *Creeds of Christendom,* 3:403). The Heidelberg Catechism answer 35 states, "That the eternal Son of God, who is, and continues true and eternal God, took upon him the very nature of man, of the flesh and blood of the Virgin Mary" (Ibid., 3:319).

entanglement in the affairs of the church. Their concern was largely justified. History demonstrates that earthly rulers in the Middle Ages oftentimes were far too involved in the affairs of the church. The rulers regularly appointed men to church office, while the churchmen dabbled in political matters outside of their domain. In addition, the church viewed the government as an arm of the church to execute those declared to be heretics. This had been done to John Hus who was condemned by the church and then burned by the magistrates.

The Anabaptists saw a similar involvement of the civil authorities in the churches of the Reformation. In Lutheranism, as noted earlier, the church tended toward Erastianism, which allowed the Christian rulers to exercise Christian discipline. In the Swiss cities, reformation came to various cantons by decision of the magistrates in the main cities. Initially, of course, all the Swiss cities were Roman Catholic. When Reformed preachers came to the cities, conflicts arose. Eventually the magistrates called for official discussions between the priests of Rome and Reformed preachers, and then a public debate was conducted. After the debate, the rulers of the city voted whether or not to go along with the Reformation. If they decided in favor of the Reformation, the priests would be expelled and the church buildings turned over to the reformers. Consequently, as also Calvin's struggles in Geneva reveal, the magistrates considered themselves a part of the governing body of the church. Anabaptists, legitimately, viewed this as improper encroachment of the government in church affairs.

However, the Anabaptists' views of the magistrate's authority went farther, crossing the boundary into radicalism. They became increasingly skeptical of all the authority of the government, and they rejected altogether the government's authority to wield the sword, to tax, and to require oaths. Many considered the government to be a necessary evil. Still others maintained that the only proper government was one that maintained the Old Testament civil laws of Moses.

It should be noted that many of the Anabaptists rejected the radical revolutionaries and their tactics. Menno Simons was one such man. Ordained a Roman Catholic priest in the Netherlands in 1524, he later confessed that at that time he had never read the Bible![23] His first struggles came over the doctrine of transubstantiation. Luther helped him here, Simons wrote, causing him "to see that human laws and commandments cannot bind to eternal death."[24] After hearing of a man executed for being rebaptized, Simons studied scripture on the matter and concluded that infant baptism had no biblical basis. Consequently, he left the Romish church.

Although he was convicted of many of the doctrinal positions of the Anabaptists, a revolutionary Simons was not. He openly reviled the radical revolutionaries Jan Matthijs and Jan of Leyden and the entire Münster rebellion. In fact, Simons came to reject the use of all force, and forbad serving in the military. His followers, known as the Mennonites quickly spread throughout the world. They formed a significant, peaceful branch of the Radical Reformation.

OTHER RADICALS

One particular group of radicals were sometimes called spiritualists because they claimed to receive special revelation from the Holy Spirit. This led to a despising of the Bible as the "dead letter," in favor of the guidance of the Spirit. Not infrequently these men

---

23 "The Conversion of Menno Simons," *Spiritual Life in Anabaptism*, ed. and trans. Cornelius J. Dyck (Scottdale, PA: Herald Press, 1995), 44.
24 Ibid., 45.

also rejected the special offices in the church, since all believers have the Spirit.

In addition, included among the radicals were rationalists. These radicals rejected anything that could not be proved by human reason. The most notable of these was Michael Servetus, a rank heretic who denied that Jesus is the Son of God and rejected the truth of the Trinity. Servetus was condemned by the Roman Catholic Church and the Reformed alike. He was eventually arrested, tried in Geneva, and burned at the stake.

The Socinians were a specific group of rationalists. They rejected justification by faith alone and questioned other cardinal doctrines, as had Servetus. Their teachings spread and gained influence in the Netherlands. Many of their views would reappear among the Arminians.

Basically, then, three kinds of radicals arose in this period: the Anabaptists, the spiritualists (claiming special revelation), and the rationalists. There was, however, much mingling and a great deal of overlap among them. The most extreme group consisted of radical revolutionaries.

How did the reformers respond to the Radical Reformation, and what effect did these radicals have on the development of the Reformation?

THE RESPONSE OF LUTHER

Martin Luther's response was emphatically negative, rejecting the radicals' teaching and their activity. As noted earlier, he condemned the peasant revolt. The entire movement, he insisted, was of the devil. Trouble arose within the Reformation over the doctrine of the Lord's supper because Luther tended to lump together as radical everyone who held a position contrary to his own. For example, Karlstadt and the Zwickau prophets rejected the physical presence of the body of Christ in the bread. The Swiss reformers (Zwingli, Bucer, Oecolampadius, and others) also took issue with Luther on this doctrine and rejected the view that Christ's body was physically present and eaten in the sacrament. Luther condemned the radicals and the Swiss reformers together. They were all "of the devil." The Radical Reformation set the stage for this division in Protestantism, and it would have momentous consequences, for it would lead to a permanent division in the Reformation between the Lutheran and Reformed branches.

On the other hand, the radical activity of Karlstadt and the Zwickau prophets in Wittenberg, described earlier, brought out a side of Luther that is not well known. It brought out the calm, pastoral spirit of the reformer. Recall that Luther came out of hiding after eleven months in the Wartburg castle. He found Wittenberg in chaos. He immediately set about to restore order in order to rescue the reformation in that city. In a series of eight masterful sermons, preached eight days in a row, Luther rebuked the radicals and restored calm to the city of Wittenberg.[25]

Luther's First Sermon, March 9, 1522

First, Luther briefly set forth the essence of the gospel. He reminded the congregation (always including himself) that we are all children of wrath, and our works are nothing. God sent his Son, and by faith in him alone we are saved. Then he went right to the point, and he admonished the congregation that we must also love. Without love, faith was nothing. He immediately added pointedly, "I see no signs of love among you." Love is not mere talk. "God does not want," insisted Luther, "hearers and repeaters of words, but followers and doers, and this occurs in faith through love."

---

25 Martin Luther, "Eight Sermons at Wittenberg 1522," in Luther's Works, vol. 51, *Sermons I*, 70–100.

That is not all that is needed—we need patience. Faith trusts in God and in his work in others. Therefore, Luther said that, "one must not insist on his rights, but must see what may be useful and helpful to his brother." He pointed out the obvious, namely, that not all members of the congregation have the same strength of faith. For this reason, we must be patient with each other. Preached Luther, "The cause is good, but there has been too much haste. For there are still brothers and sisters on the other side who belong to us and must still be won."

Specifically, he noted that under the influence of the less patient, the mass had been abolished. Luther did not consider that a bad thing in itself, but his complaint was that it was not done in an orderly way. It was done with "no regard for proper order and with offence to your neighbor."

Luther distinguished between what is a "must" (something required) and what is "free" (a choice or indifferent). Some things were musts, that is, necessary, such as faith. But he admonished the leaders that they ought not make a "must" out of what was "free." Rather, this is what ought to be done: feed the people with milk, show love to the neighbor, and have patience.

Luther's Second Sermon, March 10, 1522

Luther began by reviewing the heart of the first sermon, and reminded Wittenbergers what is the chief characteristic of a Christian, namely, that he has faith toward God and love toward the neighbor. Then he returned to the subject of the abolition of the mass and the changes in the celebration of the Lord's supper that were imposed on the congregation.

Luther readily admitted that the mass, as a sacrifice and a work of merit, was evil and had to be abolished. But how ought that to be done? Not, he maintained, by dragging people from it "by the hair." Rather, he insisted, preach the word, and "the results must be left solely to God's good-pleasure." Luther condemned forcing people to change. He pointed out that if this was done, there was no understanding or conviction on their part. "Love demonstrates that you have compassion on the weak." Luther pointed to his own example as proof of the power of the word:

> I opposed indulgences and all the papists, but never with force. I simply taught, preached, and wrote God's word; otherwise I did nothing. And while I slept, or drank Wittenberg beer with my friends...the word so greatly weakened the papacy that no prince or emperor ever inflicted such losses upon it. I did nothing; the word did everything.

Luther also pointed out the danger of making laws in the church: "One law will soon make two, and two will increase to three, and so forth."

The Third Sermon, March 11, 1522

Luther reminded the congregation of the distinction between what is a "must" and what is "free," and he applied it to marriage. He instructed them that, if a priest, monk, or nun cannot abstain, they ought to marry. But no undue pressure ought to be exerted on them, and they certainly ought not to be compelled to marry.

Concerning images, Luther taught that they are not necessary, and we are therefore free to have them in the churches or not, though it is better that we not have them. His solution to the radicals was that they should have preached that the images were nothing, Luther insisted that then "they would have fallen of themselves."

The Fourth Sermon, March 12, 1522

In the fourth sermon, Luther continued to address the matter of images in the church buildings. He maintained that if they were not being worshiped, they were nothing and did not need to be destroyed. He drew an analogy to show the absurdity of those insisting on the destruction of images: "Wine and women bring many a man to misery and make a fool of them; so we [should] kill all the women and pour out all the wine."

He turned next to the matter of eating meat on Fridays, and he noted that God has given us liberty to eat any kind of food. If you need meat (for your health's sake) eat meat, he taught. On the other hand, if the pope says you may not eat meat, then eat it to spite the pope. But, Luther maintained, the weak in faith need instruction. Our approach must be entirely different from one who is stubborn. We are to bear patiently with people who do not eat meat on Fridays, not then to use our liberty as an offense.

The Fifth Sermon, March 13, 1522

Noting that Rome's laws forbad any member from touching the elements of the sacrament of the Lord's supper, Luther was quick to point out that it is not a sin if a layman touches the elements. But then he turns on the radicals, who insisted that the people must touch the bread and the wine. That was also wrong!

In a most poignant statement, Luther indicated how serious he considered these actions of the radicals to be, and he lamented, "I dare say that none of my enemies, though they have caused me much sorrow, have wounded me as you have." Why? The reasons were obvious. These radicals had offended the weak members of the flock. They did so by forcing them to touch the bread and to partake of both bread and wine when they were not ready to do so. The members were forced, while believing that they were sinning, by handling the consecrated elements. Luther empathized with the weak members of his flock.

The Sixth through Eighth Sermons, March 14–16, 1522

In the last three sermons, Luther returned to the importance of love. He reminded the congregation that the fruit of the sacrament is love! We are to treat our neighbors as God treats us. He set before them 1 Corinthians 13 and demonstrated that they were not showing mutual love.

Luther's parting message to the radicals was: You were correct in many of the issues that you raised. But you were entirely wrong in the way you went about implementing them, for you demonstrated a lack of love and patience. You forced rather than instructed.

CALVIN AND THE RADICALS

In general it should be noted that John Calvin did not, in distinction from Luther, lump all the radicals into one group. Luther labeled them without distinction as spiritualists, fanatics, enthusiasts, and Anabaptists, even including the Swiss reformers as fanatics because of their stand on the presence of Christ in the Lord's supper.

Calvin, on the other hand, divided the radicals into two main groups. He saw that some of the radicals, namely the Libertines and the spiritualists, rejected the authority of the scriptures. Others, he wrote, "though she be full of wicked and pernicious errors, yet doth she abide in much more simplicity. For she yet receiveth the Holy Scripture, as we do."[26] These latter he would ordinarily identify as the Anabaptists. The main fault Calvin found with the Anabaptists was their failure to interpret scripture properly. He

---

26 Quoted in Willem Balke, tran. William J. Heynen, *Calvin and the Anabaptist Radicals* (Grand Rapids, MI: Wm. B. Eerdmans, 1981), 10.

also pointed out that theology requires more than merely quoting texts from the Bible.[27]

Calvin's first brush with the radicals was in eschatology, and it was not, as one might expect, with their radical view of the millennium, but with soul sleep (Karlstadt also taught this). Over against that error, the young Calvin wrote *Psychopannychia*—written around 1534–36, but not published until 1542.

Calvin's knowledge of the Anabaptists had a significant impact on his theological work. In fact, Calvin reveals in his preface to the commentary on the Psalms that a significant motivating factor for writing the *Institutes of the Christian Religion* (the first edition was published in 1536) was to defend the Protestants in France against the charge that they were Anabaptists and seditious persons.[28]

After Calvin was forced to flee from Paris due to the onset of persecution, he settled for a time in Basel, Switzerland. There he heard continued reports that "many faithful and holy persons were burnt alive in France," which news "excited the strongest disapproval of the Germans...In order to allay this indignation, certain wicked and lying pamphlets were circulated, stating that none were treated with such cruelty but Anabaptists and seditious persons, who by their perverse ravings and false opinions, were overthrowing not only religion but also all civil order." In the face of this, Calvin became convicted that, as he put it, "unless I

---

27 Calvin characterized the Anabaptists as fanatics, ignorant, deluded, poor dreamers, poor fools, foolish men, scatterbrains, without reason, unreasonable, insane, harebrained, obstinate, and poor ignoramuses. If that sounds bad, consider that the names used for the Libertines included heretics, blasphemers, scoundrels, wretches, mad dogs, and asses. Quoted in Benjamin Wirt Farley, ed. and trans., *John Calvin: Treatises against the Anabaptists and against the Libertines* (Grand Rapids, MI: Baker Book House, 1982), 30.

28 See Calvin's "Preface to the Psalms," *Calvin's Commentaries: Joshua, Psalms 1–35*, ed. and trans. Henry Beveridge (Grand Rapids, MI: Baker Book House, 1984), 4:xli, xlii.

opposed them to the utmost of my ability, my silence could not be vindicated from the charge of cowardice and treachery." He added, "This was the consideration which induced me to publish my Institute of the Christian Religion."[29] He stated his goal for writing and publishing this work:

> My objects were, first, to prove that these reports were false and calumnious, and thus to vindicate my brethren, whose death was precious in the sight of the Lord; and next, that as the same cruelties might very soon after be exercised against many unhappy individuals, foreign nations might be touched with at least some compassion towards them and solicitude about them. When it was then published, it was not that copious and labored work which it now is, but only a small treatise containing a summary of the principal truths of the Christian religion, and it was published with no other design than that men might know what was the faith held by those whom I saw basely and wickedly defamed by those flagitious and perfidious flatterers.[30]

In harmony with this purpose, the first edition of the *Institutes* was dedicated to Francis I, king of France, and the dedicatory letter revealed Calvin's intent to demonstrate to the king that the Reformation was distinct from the radicals in France. His attempt to do so is evident already in the letter, for while the Anabaptists tended to dishonor rulers, Calvin's letter, though straightforward, is deferential, giving proper honor to the king of France.[31] The

---

29 Ibid., 4:xli, xlii. The singular "Institute" is Calvin's language. He regarded it simply as "instruction" in the Christian religion.

30 Ibid., xlii.

31 This dedicatory letter to King Francis I was included in John Calvin's 1536 edition of the *Institutes of the Christian Religion*, trans. Ford Lewis Battles (Grand

address of the letter is: "For the Most Mighty and Illustrious Monarch, Francis, Most Christian King of the French, his Sovereign, John Calvin Craves Peace and Salvation in Christ."[32] In the letter Calvin refers to him with such terms as "most glorious King," "most noble King," "most invincible King," and "most serene King." The letter concludes with this desire: "May the Lord, the King of Kings, establish your throne in righteousness, and your dominion in equity, most illustrious King."[33] Compare this proper respect paid to rulers to Thomas Müntzer's address to magistrates, which we took note of earlier.

The body of the letter states in more detail what Calvin wrote in the preface to the Psalms commentary was his purpose for sending the *Institutes* to the king. In it Calvin writes as though the king is misinformed by many wicked men spreading lies about the protestants and gives a defense of their beliefs and practices.

In the first edition of the *Institutes of the Christian Religion*, Calvin is at pains to demonstrate that the Reformed are wholly different from the Anabaptists. He explicitly rejects the Anabaptists' view of the church, their practice of separation from the church, and their dividing of the church into factions with strange doctrines. He also rejected the "perfect church" notion of the Anabaptists, though he insisted on faithful Christian discipline.

On the sacraments, in general, Calvin emphasized the importance of the word. Apart from the word the sacraments have no meaning. He also affirmed the necessity of infant baptism, arguing

---

Rapids, MI: Wm. B. Eerdmans Publishing Company, 1986), 1:9–31. It is also usually included in the translations of the 1559 editions, including that of Beveridge and Battles.

32 John Calvin, "Prefatory Address to King Francis I of France," in *Institutes of Christian* Religion, ed. John T. McNeill, trans. Ford Lewis Battles (Philadelphia: Westminster Press, 1960), 9.

33 Ibid., 9–31.

especially on the basis of the unity of the two testaments and the practice of circumcising infants in the Old Testament.

Calvin addressed on the other significant errors of the Anabaptists as well: the swearing of oaths, honoring the civil government, pacifism, and paying taxes. He demonstrated that the Reformed believers disagreed with all the positions of the Anabaptists. Clearly much of the material of the very first edition of the *Institutes* was shaped by Calvin's interaction with the Anabaptists and rejection of their errors.

In the providence of God, Calvin would have other encounters with Anabaptists throughout his ministry would force him to deal explicitly with their doctrines and practices, starting with Calvin's first stay in Geneva (1536–38). Very early in his first stay, Farel and Calvin encountered opposition, and the Anabaptists from the Netherlands were included in the parties contradicting them. Disputations were held in March 1537. First Farel disputed with the Anabaptists, and twelve days later Calvin disputed with them. Even though the magistrates ruled that the reformers had demonstrated the errors of the Anabaptists and demanded that the Anabaptists must capitulate or depart from the city, the Anabaptists remained. They continued to stir up trouble for the reformers and were a partial cause of unrest that eventually led to the expulsion of Calvin and Farel from Geneva in April 1538.[34]

After leaving Geneva, Calvin desired to be finished with the pastoral ministry and enter into a life of scholarship and writing. However, Martin Bucer prevailed on him to take a pastorate of a church of French refugees in Strasbourg. Calvin pastored this refugee congregation, made up of his own countrymen, from 1538

---

34 In his "Preface to the Psalms," xliii, Calvin writes of how, only four months after he arrived in Geneva, "the Anabaptists began to assail us." He goes on to describe how this and other "certain commotions" led to his being "banished from Geneva."

to 1541. Once again, God in his providence brought Calvin into contact with the Anabaptists.

Early in the Reformation, Strasbourg had been troubled by the Anabaptists—even some of the more radical Anabaptists such as Melchior Hoffmann and Jan Matthijs.[35] Nowhere were the Anabaptists treated with more consideration than in Strasbourg. The reformers Capito and Bucer were of the opinion that the Anabaptists could be convinced by the truth and that the truth would eventually win out.

During his time in Strasbourg, Calvin labored hard and long to bring the Anabaptists back to the fold of the Reformed faith. He enjoyed much success, which can be attributed especially to three things. First, Calvin insisted that the church of which he was pastor maintain good ecclesiastical discipline. This was particularly important for the Anabaptists who reacted against the ungodliness sometimes manifested (tolerated?) in Protestant churches. Second, Calvin was a particularly effective polemicist. He was able powerfully to demonstrate the truth of the reformers over against the error of the Anabaptists. Third, Calvin was able to recognize and distinguish between those who were revolutionary and fanatical on the one hand, and those who were peaceful and devout adherents to believers' baptism on the other. As a result of his efforts, a number of Anabaptists forsook their error and rejoined the Reformed churches.

Calvin returned to Geneva in 1541 and remained there until his death in 1564. The first fifteen years of his pastorate were difficult years filled with controversy and opposition to his work. Calvin faced especially two opponents, Rome and the radicals.

---

35 Willem Balke notes that all the "Anabaptist groups shared in a common, feverish longing for the advent of the kingdom of God," which accounts for the tie to these radicals. *Calvin and the Anabaptist Radicals*, trans. William Heynen (Grand Rapids, MI: William B. Eerdmans Publishing Company, 1981), 126.

Our interest now is his writings against the radicals, which came out of his second stay in Geneva.

As noted earlier, Calvin distinguished between different groups of radicals. Against the Anabaptists he wrote in 1544 the "Brief Instruction for Arming all the Good Faithful Against the Errors of the Common Sect of the Anabaptists."[36] Calvin wrote this in response to an appeal from his close friend William Farel, who was battling the Anabaptists in Neuchatel. In this treatise, Calvin mainly dealt with the articles of the Schleitheim Confession, an Anabaptist confession published in 1527.[37] The work consisted of seven articles, largely the work of Michael Sattler. With some of the articles, Calvin had little or no disagreement. What he refuted were the Anabaptist positions on baptism; the ban; the magistrate; the oath; the incarnation; and the state of souls after death.

The whole of Calvin's treatise is worth reading, but his discussion of the ban is particularly interesting. Calvin's zeal for proper Christian discipline is well known. The Anabaptist ban, though perhaps a form of Christian discipline, differs from it greatly. Calvin raises three issues with the practice. These concerns indicate his careful analysis of the Anabaptists' documents, as well as his genuine determination to help people—also the Anabaptists themselves—grasp the errors. First, he asks, is the ban essential for the proper functioning of the church? Second, are only

---

36 John Calvin, "Brief Instruction for Arming All the Good Faithful Against the Errors of the Common Sect of the Anabaptists," in *Treatises Against the Anabaptists and Against the Libertines*, ed. and trans. Benjamin Wirt Farley (Grand Rapids, MI: Baker Book House, 1982), 36–158.

37 The seven articles of The Schleitheim Confession are: Baptism; The Ban; Breaking of Bread; Separation from the Abomination; Pastors in the Church; The Sword; The Oath. The Schleitheim Confession can be accessed at: www.anabaptists.org/history/the-schleitheim-confession.html.

unintended sins forgiven? Finally, is banishment from the congregation the true aim of discipline?

Calvin also had opportunity to write against the Libertines. Over the years, Calvin had many battles with Libertines in Geneva's congregations, some of whom were members of the city councils. But their influence was not limited to Geneva, and in 1545, at the request of several reformers, Calvin wrote a treatise entitled "Against the Fantastic and Furious Sect of the Libertines Who are Called 'Spiritualists.'" Calvin felt compelled to oppose this sect because of its growing influence and its sheer perniciousness. Benjamin Farley paraphrases Calvin's description of the error: "They teach an esoteric and pantheistic form of determinism, characterized by a crass antinomian and libertine ethic and tinged with a radical eschatology."[38]

Calvin related the errors of the Libertines of his day to the heretical view of the Gnostics (chapters 1–3). He was convinced that the movement consisted largely of people who become disenchanted with the "simplicity of the Scriptures" and indulge in "frivolous speculations." In addition, Calvin described them as "profane people" who grow tired of carrying the yoke of Christ and "want an easier moral path to follow."[39]

In chapters 7–10, Calvin criticized the spiritualist hermeneutics of the Libertines—a critique that is still pertinent today. First, he noted that their use of lofty, obscure language hinders communication and prevented clear understanding of God's word. Second, he pointed out that the Libertines gave double meaning to passages of scripture. This, he maintained, obscured God's word instead of teaching what is "clear, pure, certain, and open." Third, Calvin demonstrated that a key hermeneutical principle

---

38 Farley, *Calvin: Treatises*, 164.
39 Ibid., 175–76.

of the Libertines is a misapplication of their oft-repeated mantra, "The letter kills but the spirit gives life." This has led, maintained Calvin, to all sorts of speculation and allegory. The Libertines completely misunderstood the Spirit's role in the interpretation of scripture. Scripture and the Spirit are inseparable, and the Spirit adds nothing new to God's revelation. Calvin affirmed a central Reformation principle of interpretation, namely, that of the scripture's natural and plain sense. Finally, Calvin focused on the Libertines' conception of "Spirit," demonstrating that it was so loose that it was empty of real meaning. This has allowed the Libertines to justify evil behavior as "spiritual."[40]

The largest section of the treatise (chapters 11–22) deals with the principal doctrine of the Libertines, namely, a kind of pantheism and a determinism that enabled them to justify godless living. Calvin made it plain that he was not inventing or imagining these teachings of the Libertines. In the final two chapters, he reprints one of their pamphlets with his critique and then lists other works promoting their error.[41]

DOCTRINAL DEVELOPMENT

The existence of the radicals in the time of Calvin clearly was a means of God to promote theological development. It has been pointed out that the first edition of Calvin's *Institutes* dealt with the Anabaptist errors. The second edition (1539) included more polemics against the Anabaptists. Over the years, as Calvin periodically revised the *Institutes*, he sharpened and developed key doctrines over against the radicals.

---

40 Ibid., 176–77.
41 The lengthy, descriptive title of chapter 23 is: "Wherein What Has Been Said About Both the Style and the False and Damnable Impiety of the Libertines Is Almost Demonstrated to the Letter in a Certain Cock-and-Bull Story by Monsieur Anthony Pocquet, One of the Proponents of the Sect." Ibid., 299.

Calvin's theological development in response to the radicals began with the doctrine of God's covenant of grace. Calvin did not consider the doctrine of the covenant to be a separate topic for development in his *Institutes*, and as a result, he would not have addressed the doctrine extensively were it not for the Anabaptists' rejection of infant baptism. In answer to that error, Calvin, along with the other reformers, demonstrated that the relationship between the Old Testament (covenant) and the New Testament is that they are one covenant. This enabled them to link the circumcision of infants in the Old Testament with the baptism of infants in the New, since both were signs of the covenant and of the forgiveness of sins. Calvin, again with the other reformers, was forced to address such issues as with whom God establishes his covenant and the place of children in the covenant because of the opposition of the Anabaptists.

As one reads Calvin on the doctrine of the covenant, one is struck by the similarity of his approach, and even his language, with the Reformed confessions and with the Reformed Form for the Administration of Baptism. In fact, Calvin wrote his own form for administering baptism, largely in response to the Anabaptists, as he reminded the pastors of Geneva shortly before he died:

> In Strasbourg I also had to make a form for baptism, because the children of the Anabaptists were brought in from areas five to ten hours distant. At that time I composed this form extemporaneously. I would advise you not to change it, however, because so much depends on this.[42]

---

42 Balke, *Calvin and the Anabaptist Radicals*, 129. This "Form of Administering Baptism" is found in *Selected Works of John Calvin*, ed. and trans. Beveridge, 2:113–18.

In *The Shaping of the Reformed Baptismal Rite in the Sixteenth Century*, Reformation scholar Hughes Oliphant Old devotes a chapter to the forms used in the Reformed churches and shows how Calvin, building on the baptism forms of other reformers, developed a form that proved the necessity of infant baptism.[43] Calvin's form gave commentary on Genesis 17:7–9, 1 Corinthians 7:14, Matthew 19:13–15, and Mark 10. In his conclusion to this chapter, Old notes that while the reformers' main changes in the administration of baptism were due to their rejection of the errors found in the Romish rites, nonetheless, "the controversy with the Anabaptists played a role in shaping the Reformed baptismal rite." He summarizes the changes in these words:

> It was as a result of the controversy with the Anabaptists that the Reformers became increasingly interested in covenant theology and the importance of circumcision as a type of baptism. This emphasis had its effect on the Reformed baptism rites…[including] increasing importance to parents rather than godparents in baptism…The polemic with the Anabaptists left its mark on the Baptismal Exhortation…[which] became very long and was characterized by much theological apologetic. One had to explain very carefully why children were being baptized.[44]

From Old's history, it is obvious that the beautiful, covenantal instruction of the Reformed Form for the Administration of Baptism adopted in the Reformed churches in the Netherlands,

---

43 Hughes Oliphant Old, *The Shaping of the Reformed Baptismal Rite in the Sixteenth Century* (Grand Rapids, MI: William B. Eerdmans Publishing Company, 1992). Chapter 6 is "Further Development and Revision of the Reformed Baptism Rite, 1526–42," 145–78. His explanation of Calvin's form is especially 171–76.

44 Ibid., 177.

translated and still used in some Reformed churches in America, including the Protestant Reformed Churches, is the fruit of the controversy with the Anabaptists.

In the final edition of the *Institutes* (1559), Calvin was at pains to demonstrate that baptism is to be administered to the infants of believers "as something owed to them." He writes:

> If they are participants in the thing signified, why shall they be debarred from the sign?...Notwithstanding, the outward sign so cleaves to the word in the sacrament that it cannot be separated from it...Therefore, since the word "baptism" is applied to infants, why shall the sign, which is an appendix of the word, be denied to them? This one reason, if no others were at hand, would be quite enough to refute all those who would speak in opposition.[45]

Calvin rejected the Anabaptist argument that the New Testament records no instances of infant baptism, noting that the Bible does record the fact that families were baptized, adding, "Because infants are not excluded when mention is made of a family's being baptized, who in his senses can reason from this that they were not baptized?"[46] Then Calvin pointed out that, "if such arguments were valid, women should similarly be barred from the Lord's Supper, since we do not read that they were admitted to it in the apostolic age."[47]

Calvin, ever a pastor, took the time to point out the blessing of infant baptism, for both the parents as well as the infants

---

45 John Calvin, *Institutes of the Christian Religion*, ed. John T. McNeill, trans. Ford Lewis Battles, 2 vols., Library of Christian Classics 20–21 (Philadelphia, PA: The Westminster Press, 1960), 4.16.5, 2:1328. All the quotations from the 1559 edition are the Battles edition.
46 Ibid., 4.16.8, 2:1331.
47 Ibid.

themselves who were baptized. It "confirms the promise given to the pious parent, and declares it to be ratified that the Lord will be God not only to him but to his seed."[48] He continued:

> On the other hand, the children receive some benefit from their baptism: being engrafted into the body of the church, are somewhat more commended to the other members. Then, when they are grown up, they are greatly spurred on to an earnest zeal for worshiping God, by whom they were received as children through a solemn symbol of adoption before they were old enough to recognize him as Father.[49]

A key argument of the Anabaptists against infant baptism was that babies do not have faith. Calvin scholar Ronald S. Wallace, drawing from Calvin's commentaries, *Institutes*, and other treatises, demonstrates that "Calvin's views on infant Baptism are to an extent influenced by his very strong views on the likelihood of early regeneration of Christian children."[50]

The necessity of infant baptism was not the only area developed by Calvin in his *Institutes* in refutation of Anabaptist error. Already in the 1539 edition of the *Institutes*, Calvin expanded his treatment of the relationship between the word and the Spirit, with a separate chapter entitled, "Fanatics, Abandoning scripture and Flying Over to Revelation, Cast Down All the Principles of Godliness." Calvin strongly condemned any effort to cut the connection between the Bible and the Holy Spirit. He wrote:

---

48 Ibid., 4.16.9, 2:1332.
49 Ibid.
50 Ronald S. Wallace, *Calvin's Doctrine of the Word and Sacrament* (Grand Rapids, MI: Wm. B. Eerdmans Publishing Company, 1957), 195.

For by a kind of mutual bond the Lord has joined together the certainty of his Word and of his Spirit so that the perfect religion of the Word may abide in our minds when the Spirit, who causes us to contemplate God's face, shines; and that we in turn may embrace the Spirit with no fear of being deceived when we recognize him in his own image, namely, in the Word.

So indeed it is. God did not bring forth his Word among men for the sake of a momentary display, intending at the coming of his Spirit to abolish it. Rather, he sent down the same Spirit by whose power he had dispensed the Word, to complete his work by the efficacious confirmation of the Word.[51]

The Anabaptist errors in ecclesiology led Calvin to give ever greater emphasis to this important doctrine. This included the concepts of the visible and invisible church, the special offices, and Christian discipline. Concerning the visible church, Calvin criticized the Anabaptists' conception of the church, stating that "until the Day of Judgment, they are vainly seeking a church besmirched with no blemish."[52] Calvin pointed the Anabaptists to the early church in Corinth:

Does he [the Apostle Paul] seek to separate himself from such? Does he cast them out of Christ's Kingdom?...He not only does nothing of the sort; he even recognizes and proclaims them to be the church of Christ and the communion of saints [1 Cor. 1:2]![53]

---

51 Quoted in Balke, *Calvin and the Anabaptist Radicals*, 99.

52 Calvin, *Institutes*, 4.1.13, 2:1028.

53 Ibid., 4.1.14, 2:1028.

Over against the Anabaptists' tendency to forsake the church in a given area in order to start their own, Calvin promoted the truth of the unity of the church, and that out of it there is no salvation. Indeed, he maintained that "separation from the church is the denial of God and Christ." Accordingly, "the Lord esteems the communion of his church so highly that he counts as a traitor and apostate from Christianity anyone who arrogantly leaves any Christian society, provided it cherishes the true ministry of Word and sacraments."[54]

It becomes abundantly apparent that Calvin developed his ecclesiology not only against the errors of Rome, but also over against the errors of the Anabaptists. In this way God determined that the truth of the Reformation would develop even more than merely as a reaction against the errors of Rome.

LESSONS FOR TODAY

Surely the church today must learn from this history of the Reformation's response to the radicals. First, it should be noted that radicals are found in virtually every reform movement. The nature of a reform movement is that it attracts people dissatisfied with the status quo. They want change. They join a reform movement with that desire, not necessarily because they are interested in pure doctrine and right theology.

The Protestant Reformed Churches experienced this in the period especially from 1924 to 1953. Then too, there were people who did not understand the doctrinal issues but who simply followed a man, the capable, powerful preacher, articulate theologian, and capable pastor Herman Hoeksema. Some of these members indicated their radical spirit in intense suspicion of anyone who might criticized the Protestant Reformed Churches or

---

54 Ibid., 4.1.10, 2:1024.

their leaders. Some exhibited it in a spirit of bitterness and constant reviling of the Christian Reformed Church. Countless pages of the *Standard Bearer* will demonstrate that Rev. Hoeksema was not of this spirit. His criticisms of the Christian Reformed Church were incisive and direct, but they were fair and were not laced with animosity.

At the same time, this history reminds us that radicals are of different kinds. Some have a correct theology and are even zealous for right theology, but they lack wisdom in working with others. Besides being deficient in wisdom, they are lacking in love, and the patience that flows out of love. They attempt to force people into conformity, rather than instruct and wait patiently for change. They cannot distinguish between things that must be changed immediately and those that ought to come gradually.

The theology of some radical is simply erroneous. These often belong to the movement for a time but later reveal their wrong understandings and their refusal to bow before scripture. This may come out in a godless walk of life, in their promoting their wrong theology, or in a form of rationalism that sets aside the teaching of scripture.

The radical spirit of the Anabaptists sought a pure church. They condemned all existing churches, including the Lutheran and Reformed churches. The same radical spirit is found today in those who tout their own church or denomination as the only true church.

The radical Thomas Müntzer believed that he could identify the elect. This radical spirit reveals itself in churches where members condemn everyone who is not in complete agreement with them or their church. The condemnation can sound very much like a judgment as to the eternal state of those who are not in agreement with them.

This radical spirit is evident in a failure to distinguish the enemy when wielding the sword. The church on earth is a militant church, called to fight the battles of the Lord, even as Israel of old. The sword of the Spirit must be taken in hand and used. However, those wielding the sword do not always act in wisdom, love, or patience. They can fail to distinguish those who are clear and obvious enemies of God—the Goliaths of this world—as opposed to those who are of the church of God but walking in, even promoting, error. The sword of the Spirit must be used against both, but in a discriminating way.

Clearly, God has determined that radicals will ever be a part of the church on earth. God has his purposes with them, serving the good of the church. As was true of the Reformation, radicals in the church force the church to develop the truth ever more sharply. Also, forewarned, the church must be on guard against the one-sidedness of radicals. Sometimes God's purposes with radicals are particularly hard, for radicals can drive members, Christians, away from the church. It does not excuse a radical member for pushing another member out of the church through his radical, unloving, impatient behavior, yet this may be how God, in his perfect wisdom, uses radicals. As in all things, God's ways are higher than our ways and beyond our comprehension.

What then is the proper, biblical response to radicals and radicalism? Let it be, first of all, that of the zealous pastor Martin Luther. Let the church reject the radicals, yet demonstrate love and patience in dealing with them. Second, the church should learn from John Calvin's approach. Make the necessary distinctions between the various groups of people who oppose the truth in various ways. On the one hand, there are those who teach errors, "wicked and pernicious errors," but respect the Bible as God's authoritative word. Reformed believers can work with these people. On the other hand, there are those who despise the word of God and refuse to bow before it. Along with Calvin the church today must clearly reject the radicals' doctrines and practices that conflict with scripture and the Reformed confessions. Scripture and the confessions are authoritative in the church.

The church today has a calling to guard against radicalism in the congregation. Indeed each member must be on guard against the spirit of radicalism in his or her own soul and life. The church must not tolerate indiscriminate condemnation of all outside the congregation. She must rebuke and restrain those who lack patience and love for visitors or fellow members. The Canons of Dordt set forth the calling to exercise the judgment of charity—an expression originating with John Calvin.[55] The church must make her continual prayer one for wisdom and courage: courage to stand for the truth of God uncompromisingly, and wisdom to do so properly out of the motive of love—for the fellow believer and, above all, for the glory of God.

---

55 The Canons say that "with respect to those who make an external profession of faith and live regular lives, we are bound…to judge and speak of them in the most favorable manner." Canons of Dordt, 3–4.15, in Schaff, *Creeds of Christendom*, 3:591.

Chapter 6

THE REFORMATION'S PROGRESS
IN THE LOWLANDS

Rev. Steven Key

≋

> But ye shall receive power, after that the Holy Ghost
> is come upon you: and ye shall be witnesses unto me both
> in Jerusalem, and in all Judaea, and in Samaria,
> and unto the uttermost part of the earth.
>
> —ACTS 1:8

"The people that walked in darkness have seen a great light: they that dwell in the land of the shadow of death, upon them hath the light shined." The fulfillment of that prophecy of Isaiah 9:2, ushered in with the incarnation of our Lord Jesus Christ, is a fulfillment that has continued with Christ's work in gathering his church throughout the New Testament age. Belonging to that glorious work of the now-exalted Christ is the work of the great Reformation of the sixteenth century. Also in the Lowlands of Europe Christ worked powerfully, wonderfully, and irresistibly, gathering his church even in the face of tremendous opposition from the powers of darkness.

When we consider the Reformation's progress in the Lowlands

from the onset of the great Reformation through the sixteenth century, we are considering our Dutch heritage as Reformed churches. *Netherlands*, after all, means "lowlands." But in the time frame that we are considering, the Netherlands under the Habsburg dynasty was a geo-political entity covering the entire region of the Low Countries, seventeen provinces that would include not only the present-day Netherlands, but also Belgium, Luxembourg, and even the very northern part of France.[1] That was true for about one hundred years, from 1482 to 1581.

In addition, for roughly the first forty years of the Reformation, the Lowlands was under the rule of the man known as the Holy Roman Emperor, Charles V, who inherited a Spanish and Habsburg empire embracing not only Spain and the Lowlands, but a large portion of Europe. It was only in the early years of the Eighty Years' War (1568–1648) that the southern provinces of the Lowlands became separated from the northern provinces. The northern provinces, roughly modern-day Netherlands, united as a Protestant nation, while the southern provinces continued under the control of the kingdom of Spain and its Roman Catholic influence. Thus in the period that we consider, I speak of the Lowlands for the sake of accuracy.[2]

This is our heritage and the history of Christ's work, a wonderful work, a work of reformation and renewal.

As we look at the progress of the Reformation in the Lowlands, I will present, first of all, an overview of the history of that progress; and then the progress as it came to expression in the

---

1   John T. Mc Neill, *The History and Character of Calvinism* (1954; repr., New York, NY: Oxford University Press, 1957), 256.

2   While I might refer occasionally to the Netherlands or use quotations that refer to the same, I will be generally referring in the broader sense of that term to the Lowlands.

Reformed confessions and the development of a Reformed church government.

HISTORY OF THE REFORMATION
IN THE LOWLANDS

Maurice Hansen, in his book *The Reformed Church in the Netherlands*, makes a helpful division of the years involving the Reformation's progress in the Netherlands. He divides the formative period of the Reformation in the Lowlands into three parts.

He first points to a period of preparation. In the handiwork of God's providence certain persons and events in the Lowlands can be pointed to as serving the unfolding of God's work in the Reformation. Those persons and events covered a period of more than two hundred years, from 1340 to 1562. That was followed by a brief period of consolidation, 1562–68. The third division of the formative period of the Reformation took place from 1568 to 1581, during which time the church in the Lowlands was finally organized and established.[3]

In the years prior to the great Reformation the need for reform within the Roman Catholic Church was recognized by many. Not only was the corruption of doctrine abhorrent, but the immorality in the church, including among the clergy, was so widespread that the times were reminiscent of the days of Eli's two sons, Hophni and Phinehas. First Samuel 2 records that their wicked abuse of the priesthood caused the people to abhor the offering of the Lord (v. 17). God used the apostasy of the Roman Catholic Church to instill in many a longing for reform and to pave the way for the wide acceptance, also in the Lowlands, of the

---

3 Maurice G. Hansen, *The Reformed Church in the Netherlands: Traced From A.D. 1340 to A.D. 1840 in Short Historical Sketches* (New York, NY: Board of Publication of the Reformed Church in America, 1884), 15.

fundamental teachings of Martin Luther and then the reformers who followed him.

Within a year after the date in 1517 that we commemorate as the beginning of the great Reformation, monks of the Augustinian order to which Luther himself had belonged had gone through various parts of the Lowlands preaching the doctrines of holy scripture.[4] "In May 1519, Erasmus wrote to Thomas Wolsey, from Antwerp, that Luther's works were circulating 'everywhere' in the Low Countries."[5] By 1522, Luther's German translation of the New Testament had also been translated into Dutch. "In August 1525, Erasmus reported that most of the 'Hollanders, Zeelanders, and Flemish knew the doctrines of Luther.'"[6]

The sympathy for Luther's teachings was found among not only the common people, but the scholars and priests as well. "In Friesland alone the priests of more than fifty villages were deposed by the Duke of Alva and banished for their suspected attachment to Luther."[7] Among the common people of the Lowlands multitudes longed for deliverance from the bondage of the Roman Catholic Church and its political attachment to Emperor Charles V, an avowed enemy of the Reformation.

We do well, in considering the development of the churches of the Reformation in the Lowlands, not to overlook the tremendous difference in the lives of God's people five centuries ago in comparison to the lives that we live today.

The population of the major cities at that time was but a small

---

4   Peter Y. De Jong, ed., *Crisis in the Reformed Churches: Essays in Commemoration of the Great Synod of Dort, 1618–1619* (Grand Rapids, MI: Reformed Fellowship, Inc., 1968).

5   Jonathan I. Israel, *The Dutch Republic: Its Rise, Greatness, and Fall 1477–1806* (New York, NY: Oxford University Press, 1995), 79.

6   Ibid., 80.

7   Hansen, *Reformed Church*, 36.

fraction in comparison to the population of those cities today. Amsterdam, for example, with a population of roughly 850,000 people today, was a city of 11,000 in 1520. By 1600, it had grown significantly to about 60,000. Yet while we might consider these small populations, the Lowlands had the most densely populated cities in Europe. "In all, nineteen Netherlands towns had a population of more than 10,000; in the whole of the British Isles there were only four."[8]

At the same time, the people faced tremendous hardships that are difficult for us to comprehend five hundred years later. There was wealth in a port city such as Antwerp, where trade flourished. But many throughout the Lowlands lived at a very low level of subsistence. The food supply was insufficient for the population. Poverty was worse in the more sizeable cities of the southern Lowlands than anywhere else in Europe.[9]

Furthermore, if a father and mother brought forth five children, they would likely have carried two of them to the cemetery in infancy, and a third before reaching maturity.[10] Women dying in childbirth was a frequent occurrence.

The Lowlands were continually under threat of invasion, and war raged almost constantly in the sixteenth century. The seventeen provinces of the Lowlands were not unified and were only nominally under the rule of the Spanish Empire. Besides the threat of invasion from enemies without, the Lowlands had a long history of mutual hostility. It was not until 1549 that the provinces were somewhat consolidated by the signing of "a document known as the 'Pragmatic Sanction', which insured that, after

---

8 Geoffrey Parker, *The Dutch Revolt* (London, England: Penguin Books, 1977), 23.
9 Ibid., 26.
10 Will Durant, *The Story of Civilization: Part VI, The Reformation: A History of European Civilization from Wyclif to Calvin: 1300–1564* (New York, NY: Simon and Schuster, 1957), 751.

the emperor's death, all the provinces would continue to obey the same ruler and the same central institutions."[11] But the political turbulence continued for decades, and the safety of the people was never insured during this history.

PERSECUTION IN THE LOWLANDS

In addition, persecution hung like a dark cloud over those who had embraced the cause of the Reformation. This was a period of time when there was no freedom of speech. The imperial edict restricted anyone from publishing anything without the approval of the authorities, and specifically the Roman Catholic authorities, that is, the bishop of that given area.

The bloody Spanish Inquisition was active in parts of the Lowlands, especially those under the direct influence of Roman Catholic authorities. This institution of the Roman Catholic Church for combating heresy by force, an institution that began already back in the twelfth century, was joined to the state under Charles V in 1522, not long after eighty books by Martin Luther were found in Leuven (Belgium). Not satisfied with the results of burning the "offensive" books of Luther, the papal nuncio "proposed to the emperor the burning of some Lutherans" also.[12] The next year "the first Protestant martyrs in the Lowlands," Henry Voes and Johann Eck, were burned at the stake in Brussels.[13]

But the regional tribunals of the Inquisition were limited by lack of manpower and resources. The persecution, therefore, only gradually increased. In April 1550, the crown issued an edict "laying down the death sentence and confiscation of all goods for heresy and distributing heretical literature."[14] Men found guilty

---

11 Parker, *Dutch Revolt*, 30.
12 Mc Neill, *Calvinism*, 257.
13 Durant, *Reformation*, 633.
14 Israel, *Dutch Republic*, 99.

and who confessed were to be beheaded, women buried alive. Those who remained obstinate and refused to confess were to be tortured until they confessed or burned at the stake. Multitudes perished; many others fled.

To those who are of Reformed background the most familiar victim among the multitudes of those who were martyred at this time was Guido de Brés, the author of the Belgic Confession of Faith. In 1556, De Brés, along with many other children of the Reformation, fled the persecution in the Lowlands by moving to Frankfurt, Germany. There he became acquainted with John Calvin and moved to Geneva to study under Calvin and Theodore Beza. In 1559 he returned to the Lowlands to minister to the persecuted churches there, but within two years he had to escape for his life to France. He served in France for about five years as a pastor to several Huguenot churches, as well as frequently traveling in secret to minister in the Lowlands. But in 1567, De Brés was arrested and imprisoned in Doornik, brought back to Valciennes (Dutch: Valencijn), France (just across the border), and martyred for Christ's sake. He was put to death by hanging in the public square. This, mind you, was a full fifty years after the beginning of the Reformation.

The intensity of the persecution in the Lowlands through those years was often a response of the government against the repeated rioting and iconoclasm of some from the sect of the Anabaptists. Many, including the rulers, identified the Reformed believers with the radical Anabaptists. Some did this out of ignorance of the distinction between them, others despite the distinction between them.

When we consider the Reformation's progress in the Lowlands, we should recognize that initially the growth of the Reformation came among those who did not fully understand the doctrines upon which the Reformation was grounded, but who were united in their opposition to the Roman Catholic Church. That opposition came for a multitude of different reasons—spiritual, economic, and political. Not only were there many whose disgust at the immorality among the leadership of the Roman Catholic Church moved them to embrace any appearance of reform, but perhaps even more influential in the rejection of the Roman Catholic hierarchy was resentment for Rome's political influence in the empire, as well as its intolerable oppression of the fiercely independent people of the Lowlands.

The lack of true spiritual knowledge, the knowledge of the scriptures, together with these other factors are the reasons why the Anabaptists had such a strong influence in the Lowlands. By rejecting the teachings of the Roman Catholic Church entirely, including the sacrament of baptism administered to infants, the Anabaptists were deemed by many to be the more thorough reformers of the church.

There were, however, broad differences among the Anabaptists, and the movement suffered from many disputes and divisions. This fragmentation of the movement prevented it from having a general and lasting influence in the Lowlands and enabled the Reformed churches to gain the dominant foothold in the years following the Reformation.[15]

Menno Simons (c. 1496–1561), who renounced the priesthood to lead a Dutch Anabaptist movement, taught nonviolent reform consisting of obedience, inner purity, and a separation from the world. Holding to many unbiblical doctrines, he became a powerful influence in the northern Lowlands and north Germany, with many of his followers becoming known as "Mennonites."

---

15 On the fragmentation of the movement, confer Israel, *Dutch Republic*, 84–96.

But among the Anabaptists were also those who not only held to various doctrinal errors, but also rejected civil authority.[16] Identifying themselves as children of the Reformation, "true reformers," they would take up arms to assist God in overthrowing their ungodly rulers. This militant branch of the Anabaptists rejected the Roman Catholic magistrates, entered the churches of Rome and destroyed them, and in many cases even attempted to take over the rule of cities. This mob violence was often joined by those who had no religious motivations in doing so, but for whom social unrest gave expression to their anti-Roman-Catholic and anti-government sentiments.

During the reign of Charles V some two thousand people in the Lowlands were executed for their rejection of Roman Catholicism.[17] The Dutchman Martin Micronius described it this way in a letter to Heinrich Bullinger dated August 28, 1550: "The same Spanish tyrant is harassing the Low Countries with the most cruel persecutions. He has established the most sanguinary [bloodthirsty] Spanish inquisition, which drives our countrymen to seek refuge in England."[18]

There is a reason why Guido de Brés in writing the Belgic Confession of Faith spoke with such vehemence when he said in article 36, "We detest the error of the Anabaptists and other seditious people, and in general all those who reject the higher powers and magistrates and would subvert justice."[19] The Protestant

---

16 A rather concise summary of the revolutionary actions of the radical Anabaptists is found in P.Y. De Jong, *The Church's Witness to the World* (St. Catherines, Ontario, Canada: Paideia Press, 1980), 35–43.

17 Parker, *Dutch Revolt*, 37.

18 Hastings Robinson, ed., *Original Letters Relative to the English Reformation, Written During the Reign of King Henry VIII, King Edward VI, and Queen Mary: Chiefly from the Archives of Zurich*, the Second Portion (Cambridge: The University Press, 1847), 568.

19 Belgic Confession 36, in Schaff, *Creeds of Christendom*, 3:433.

reformers and Reformed believers suffered enormously during the early years of the Reformation in the Lowlands because they were associated with the Anabaptists. The threat of persecution was real. Humanly speaking, there were all kinds of deterrents to the study of God's word and the writings of the reformers, let alone the publication of those writings, and even more, to following the cause of the Reformation.

Imagine breathing the stench of the burnt corpses of your pastors, those who had been unfolding to you the truth of the gospel. Imagine facing the torture of the rack, and witnessing the gallows being used for the innocent. Imagine women being drowned in the cold waters of the Lowlands.[20] Think about how Satan could torment the minds of God's people during that period when it seemed that there was no relief in sight. Then you can begin to sense the wonder of God's grace at work in this period of the church's history in the Lowlands.

THE SPREAD OF THE REFORMED FAITH IN THE LOWLANDS

There was one noteworthy strength in the Lowlands in the sixteenth century. In 1549, the crown prince, Philip, son and heir of Emperor Charles V, paid a state visit to his father's possession in the Lowlands, where he "noted the widespread literacy" of the people and the flourishing educational system.[21] All the way back

---

20 A number of instances of martyrdom are recorded by Gerard Brandt in volume I, Book IV of *The History of the Reformation and Other Ecclesiastical Transactions In and About the Low-Countries, From the Beginning of the Eighth Century, Down to the Famous Synod of Dort, Inclusive* (1720; repr., New York, NY: AMS Press, Inc., 1979).

21 Parker, *Dutch Revolt*, 21. The educational system in the Lowlands developed under God's providence by the influence of a pre-reformer, Gerhard Groote (1340–84). Groote was determined to make education prepare the way for religion, and he applied himself to the development of the educational system in the

to the late fourteenth century, under the influence of one who might be considered a pre-reformer, Gerhard Groote, education became a matter of emphasis. Schools were established in several cities of the Lowlands and found healthy support among the people.[22]

This strength of education would eventually play an important role in the development of the Reformation in the Lowlands. Geoffrey Parker in his book *The Dutch Revolt* states, "In the sixteenth century book-learnin' led to Calvinism."[23] God used that, in part, to draw his people to the gospel once again, as the truth restored by Luther and the other reformers was widely read and embraced.

The writings of Luther, the instruction of other reformers, and the preaching of faithful ministers laid the doctrinal foundation of this unfolding work of the Holy Spirit in the church.

In addition, Gerard Brandt, in his history of the Reformation, gives account of the influence of the French Psalter compiled by Clement Marot and Theodore Beza. People would gather in the streets to sing the psalms, exasperating their persecutors. There were many occasions when those who were being executed for their faith sang the psalms and were joined by the crowd witnessing their execution.[24]

But growth in doctrinal understanding took time, as did the development of any institutional structure for Protestant and Reformed churches in the Lowlands. That was true especially

---

Lowlands. Cf. Richard R. De Ritter, *A Survey of the Sources of Reformed Church Policy and the Form of Government of the Christian Reformed Church in America*, class syllabus (Grand Rapids, MI: Calvin Theological Seminary, 1983), 22–23.

22 Hansen, *Reformed Church*, 18–21. This important influence of education is also referred to by Mc Neill, *Calvinism*, 255.

23 Parker, *Dutch Revolt*, 21.

24 Brandt, *History of the Reformation*, 1:137.

when the persecution compelled many of the leading lights of the Reformation to flee for refuge to the English capital of London; Emden, in East Friesland (Ostfriesland), Germany; Wezel, Germany; and other places where they could find relative safety, a few even making their way to Geneva.[25] For a period of about thirty years, fugitives from the persecution in the Lowlands found refuge and blessed hospitality in these cities of refuge.[26]

The influence of John Calvin came rather late to the Lowlands.[27] Calvin himself was a second-generation reformer following the path marked out by Martin Luther, Ulrich Zwingli, Martin Bucer, and other reformers who had brought to the church

---

25 A. C. Duke, Gillian Lewis, Andrew Pettegree, eds., *Calvinism in Europe, 1540-1610: A Collection of Documents* (New York, NY: St. Martin's Press, 1992), 129.

26 Hansen, *Reformed Church*, 67, notes the public acknowledgment given to the city of Wezel for the hospitality the refugees had received there. "An oration was delivered in their name, addressed to the members of the town council, in which mention was made of the kindness with which already for thirty years past the city had taken the strangers from the Netherlands to itself, as to an asylum. Its houses had been opened to them; for their protection the citizens had exposed themselves to disfavor and even to danger; their infirmities had been borne with patience; they had been aided with counsel and substance; they had been delivered from discomforts; the citizens had been to them as father and mother, relatives and friends. 'Your city,' said the orator, 'has truly been to us a fatherland, because we were permitted with you to live and die, and with you to worship God in spirit and in truth.'"

27 I would note in this connection that John Calvin, although a Frenchman, is on record as saying, "I am a Dutchman myself." The remark was occasioned by the procrastination of a young man from the Lowlands. Calvin's fellow reformer Heinrich Bullinger had sent a very important letter to Calvin, relying on a Dutchman to deliver it. The young messenger, upon arriving in Geneva, took five more days to deliver the letter to Calvin. Calvin attempted to quiet the disturbed Bullinger by saying, "I am used to the barbarity of this neighboring people," adding as a bit of humor, "I am a Dutchman myself." (Machiel A. Van den Berg, *Friends of Calvin*, trans. Reinder Bruinsma [Grand Rapids, MI: William B. Eerdmans Publishing Company, 2009], 186). If it's any comfort to the Dutch, the Latin expression he used was *Sum enim Belga ipse quoque.* So he was referring specifically to that area of the Lowlands of which the people were Belgian. Since Calvin came from northern France, he was acquainted with the Belgian people.

a renewed emphasis on expository preaching and the restoration of biblical truth.

Calvin's wife, Idelette, was of Walloon origin. She and her first husband had fled the city of Liège in the Belgic region of Wallonia and had come as refugees to Strasbourg. There under the influence of Reformed preaching they forsook the Anabaptist errors for the Reformed faith. "In Strasbourg and later in Geneva many other French-speaking Netherlanders learned Calvinism or were confirmed in it."[28] Meanwhile, in the north, Dutch-speaking Lowlanders were embracing the Reformed faith as taught by the Polish reformer John à Lasco and other faithful ministers in Emden and other areas of East Friesland.[29]

While we commemorate the origin of the Reformation in 1517, there were no established Reformed, that is, Calvinistic churches in the Lowlands until nearly forty years later. While there were over seven hundred fifty Reformed churches in France in 1561, there were only about twenty in the Lowlands. In the following five years, however, as persecution increased in France, many Calvinists took refuge in the southern Lowlands and the number of churches increased dramatically.[30]

In his providence, God saw to the spread of Calvinism in the Lowlands, using largely the influence of the Walloon congregations in the French-speaking region of what is now southern Belgium. These scattered Calvinistic congregations, meeting secretly because of the persecution, gave themselves to the spread of the Reformed faith.

---

28 Mc Neill, *Calvinism*, 259.
29 John Calvin dedicated his Latin Catechism of 1545 "to the faithful ministers of Christ throughout East Friesland." Israel examines the influence especially of John à Lasco in the development of the Reformed faith in the Lowlands (*Dutch Republic*, 101–5).
30 Parker, *Dutch Revolt*, 58.

In addition, God used the labors of four preachers in the spread of the gospel embodied in the Reformed faith of Calvin throughout the Lowlands. Those four were Guido de Brés, Peter Dathenus, Herman Strijcker, who was often known under his Hebrew name Moded, and Franciscus Junius.[31]

In the spring of 1566, under pressure from more than three hundred of her nobles, the regent, Margaret of Parma, issued a decree effectively suspending the Inquisition in the Lowlands.[32] Almost immediately hundreds of people who had fled the Lowlands to escape persecution returned home, including some fifty Calvinist preachers.[33] Most came into the southern Lowlands from churches in France and Switzerland. The south was largely French or Flemish speaking, and the ministers in this area corresponded especially with the churches in France and Geneva, while the north was predominantly Dutch speaking and had closer relations with the churches in London and Germany.[34]

In that way a Reformed man such as Guido de Brés bore influence especially in the southern Lowlands with his Confession of Faith, which was itself modeled after the French Confession of

---

31 Hansen, *Reformed Church*, 55–56. We are familiar with De Brés (1522–67) as the author of the Belgic Confession. Dathenus (c. 1531–88) made great contributions in translating the Heidelberg Catechism into the Dutch language and preparing Dutch versifications of the psalms, as well as preparing the liturgical forms later adopted for use in the Reformed Churches in the Netherlands. Herman Moded (c. 1520–1603), whose Dutch name was Herman Strijcker (sometimes also referred to as Herman Modet), was minister in the Reformed Church of Antwerp from 1560 to 1566 and a major contributor to the growth of Calvinism in Antwerp. He also was influential by boldly preaching in other places for the spread of the gospel. Junius (1545–1602) also became a leading figure in the developing Reformed churches in the Lowlands. When he died in 1602, he was a professor of theology in the University of Leyden.

32 Ibid., 56–57.

33 Phyllis Mack Crew, *Calvinist Preaching and Iconoclasm in the Netherlands, 1544–1569* (Cambridge, England: Cambridge University Press, 1978), 1.

34 Ibid.

Faith written by Calvin. At the same time the Heidelberg Catechism of Zacharias Ursinus and Caspar Olevianus was used by God especially in the northern Lowlands to establish the truth of the scriptures known as the Reformed faith. The Belgic Confession of Faith of De Brés, originally published in 1561 in the French language for the churches in the southern Lowlands, soon joined the Heidelberg Catechism as influential also in the northern Lowlands, as in 1562 it was also translated into the Dutch language for the churches in the northern provinces.[35] The Reformed confessions, therefore, played a significant role in the progress of the Reformation in the Lowlands.

THE ROLE OF THE CONFESSIONS

Among the Reformed churches not only expository preaching was greatly emphasized in the churches' labors, but also catechism instruction and mission work by means of catechism instruction. The Reformed confessions were embraced early as instruments of such instruction.

But the confessions were also important in laying the foundation for the institutional formation of the Reformed churches in the Lowlands. The unity of the church, after all, is a unity based upon the truth of the scriptures. Simply to abandon the apostate Roman Catholic Church was not reformation. In fact, as the Anabaptists demonstrated, simple abandonment and rejection of error leads to chaos if there is not true reform according to the word of God. Ignorance abounded at that time, no less than ignorance abounds five hundred years later. Various sects were found throughout the Lowlands, and heresies abounded. Many of

---

35 Hansen, *Reformed Church*, 59.

the leaders of new congregations saw firsthand the importance of basic instruction in the truths of the scriptures.[36]

Besides their role in providing individual instruction, a confessional foundation had to be laid for the newly Reformed churches, that congregations might be not only established, but unified in the truth of holy scripture. De Brés himself recognized that, as he wrote to the consistory in Antwerp in 1565: "It is desired to bring us into accord with the Germans in one Confession...so as to break the power of the pope utterly...It would also serve to shut the mouths of those who say we are not unified."[37] One church historian writes, "It is no stretch to argue that the Reformed church could hardly have survived without such confessional and doctrinal codification."[38] The Reformed churches in the Lowlands were established as confessional churches.

The Belgic Confession and the Heidelberg Catechism only received their official place as the adopted doctrinal standards of the Reformed churches in the Lowlands at the Synod of Dordt, 1618–19. But already in 1561 at a synod of the Walloon churches held in Antwerp, the Belgic Confession was recognized as a faithful expression of the historic faith of the holy scriptures. Franciscus Junius' autobiography,[39] reflecting on his position as clerk of the Synod of Antwerp in 1566, indicates that already then the Belgic Confession was recognized as a standard of unity for

---

36 Confer the letter of Gasper vander Heyden, leader of the new congregation in Antwerp, 1555. Duke, Lewis, and Pettegree, *Calvinism in Europe*, 133–36.

37 Quoted in Crew, *Calvinist Preaching*, 83.

38 Willem J. Van Asselt, *Introduction to Reformed Scholasticism*, trans. Albert Gootjes (Grand Rapids, MI: Reformation Heritage Books, 2011), 109.

39 Franciscus Junius, *A Treatise on True Theology, with the Life of Franciscus Junius*, trans. David C. Noe (Grand Rapids, MI: Reformation Heritage Books, 2014). Junius was a student in Geneva, arriving in 1562 and studying there until agreeing in 1565 to serve as pastor in Antwerp. He was examined by the Genevan church council and deemed worthy of the pastorate. (See Crew, *Calvinist Preaching*, 86.)

the churches.[40] In 1568 a number of Reformed ministers gathered in Wesel in preparation for organizing the churches in the Lowlands. The ministers "determined that agreement with the Belgic Confession was to be a prerequisite for admission to the public ministry in the churches."[41]

What these ministers had determined became the official position of the churches three years later at the Synod of Emden (1571). This synod of the Reformed churches in the Lowlands was held at Emden in Germany because it was not yet safe to meet in the Lowlands. Here the authority of the Belgic Confession was affirmed and the decision taken to require subscription of the ministers in order to maintain doctrinal agreement within the Dutch churches. The churches of the Lowlands "would be confessionally Reformed."[42]

These confessions breathed the truth of the scriptures. Therefore, they not only served the development of the Reformed churches in the Lowlands, but also established their roots with the church historically, demonstrating that the Reformation was a return to and continuation of the historic, catholic Christian faith. It was, in fact, the restoration of the apostolic faith.

When it is remembered that these confessions arose out of the intense persecution of those early years, when the personal and experiential approach of the authors of both the Heidelberg Catechism and the Belgic Confession is also recalled, then the evidence of God's abounding grace during this time is underscored.

---

40 Nicolaas H. Gootjes, *The Belgic Confession: Its History and Sources* (Grand Rapids, MI: Baker Academic, 2007), 97–99.
41 Ibid., 100.
42 Ibid., 100–102. At the provincial Synod of Dordt, 1574, the requirement of subscription was extended to the elders and deacons as well. In 1581, at the National Synod Middleburg, professors of theology as well as school teachers were added to that requirement. See ibid., 103–4.

The same is true of the liturgical forms of the Reformed churches in the Lowlands, which were also written during this period of the Reformation's progress. Peter Dathenus, while in exile in the Palatinate community of Frankenthal, used his time there compiling a "Flemish translation of the psalms and a new Reformed liturgy," including "the forms for baptism" and the Lord's supper. These forms are essentially still in use in our churches today, as well as the form for marriage. These forms were all later adopted by the Reformed churches in the Netherlands to be used in the congregations.[43] They all have their roots in this early period of the Reformation in the Lowlands.

THE DEVELOPMENT OF
REFORMED CHURCH ORDER

The progress of the Reformation in the Lowlands was also seen in the development of Reformed church order. This also was a critically important element of the developments in the Lowlands. Contributing to this was the recognition of the importance of a trained ministry as well as the need for the various Reformed congregations throughout the Lowlands to unify and to express their unity in a denomination established in a confessional Reformed faith.

The need for a faithful ministry, bound by the Reformed confessions and committed to the truth of scripture, functioning according to a Reformed church order, was pressing. Ignorance of the scriptures and the Reformed faith, compromise and neglect, characterized many village pastors. Jonathan Israel, in his book *The Dutch Republic*, cites certain examples:

---

43 Crew, *Calvinist Preaching*, 103. See also B. Wielenga, *The Reformed Baptism Form: A Commentary*, ed. David J. Engelsma, trans. Annemie Godbehere (Jenison, MI: Reformed Free Publishing Association, 2016), 7.

The pastor at Doorn was reported to have been a Catholic priest during the 1570's, Reformed after the collapse of Spanish power in 1576 but, "through fear of the enemy", somewhere in between since the Spanish revival, in the 1580's. The pastor at Werkhoven was reported to be only "slightly" Reformed but willing to do better. At Odijk, the pastor had thrown out some images but retained others, and performed Catholic and Reformed baptisms and marriages, according to parishioners' preferences. At Houten, the preacher was simply hopelessly ignorant about the old faith and the new.[44]

In addition, the leaders of the Reformation in the Lowlands also understood that to establish and maintain the unity of the church, the instruction of God's word must be heeded. "Let all things be done decently and in order" (1 Cor. 14:40). "For God is not the author of confusion, but of peace, as in all churches of the saints" (v. 33).

In the early years of the Reformation in the Lowlands, there was little structure to the church. Persecution contributed to that. But in many locations people met in small gatherings led by men with little or no formal theological training. In some instances these men who led worship services had only read some of the writings of Luther.

During the intense persecution taking place in the Lowlands, many Reformed Christians fled to London and to Germany. There they received important influences that would prove helpful in the establishment of the Reformed churches in the Lowlands upon a biblical form of church government. With foresight some made provision for the time when God would see to the unification of

---

44 Israel, *Dutch Republic*, 364–65.

the scattered congregations under the cross of persecution and the establishment of a Reformed denomination in the Lowlands. While in London laboring with John á Lasco, Martin Micronius[45] translated Á Lasco's church order and liturgical forms into the Dutch language, introducing them to the Dutch refugees in London.[46]

There were occasional ecclesiastical assemblies held in secret in the south during the 1550s, but for the most part, questions of church government and discipline were addressed by correspondence rather than assemblies. The Dutch churches did not hesitate to seek the advice of other reformers or Reformed churches, whether in London, Emden, Geneva, or elsewhere. The Italian Reformed theologian Peter Martyr Vermigli gave advice in at least one case involving a Dutch Reformed pastor who had shown sympathies to Anabaptist error denying Christ's incarnation.[47]

The French-speaking churches of the southern Lowlands were the first to gather as a synod. The Walloon churches held a synod in Antwerp in 1561, as well as in 1566, where the Belgic Confession was first adopted as the official confessional standard for the churches.

The first steps toward an official assembly of the Dutch-

---

45 Micronius received the highest commendation as a minister in a letter from John Utenhovius to Henry Bullinger: "The word, however, is proclaimed in all its purity, with the greatest benefit to the church, by our friend Martin Micronius, who preaches in a popular manner, like the clergy at Zurich, and is at the same time a cautious interpreter of the word, introducing nothing that is forced or trifling, and which does not tend to entire edification." Robinson, *Original Letters*, 587.

46 "Micronius, Martin," *McClintock and Strong Biblical Cyclopedia*, accessed February 20, 2018, citation from http://www.biblicalcyclopedia.com/M/micronius-martin.html.

47 Peter Martyr Vermigli, *The Peter Martyr Library; ser. 1, v. 5, Life, Letters, and Sermons*, ed. and trans. John Patrick Donnelly, S. J. (Kirksville, MO: Thomas Jefferson University Press, 1999), 184–97.

speaking Reformed churches in the northern Lowlands were taken when about forty ministers and elders, apparently under the leadership of Peter Dathenus, met in the German town of Wezel in the fall of 1568. This assembly was not one of any binding authority, because the officebearers in attendance were not delegated by the churches with any authority to make binding decisions. But there they drafted the basis of a church order, as advice to the churches until such time as a general synod could be held to make official decisions about such matters.

The opening decisions of this assembly indicate the mind of those gathered concerning the importance of a trained, godly ministry and an established denominational unity in doctrine, organization, worship practices, and discipline.

(1) Inasmuch as it will be especially necessary, first of all, for the proper regulation of the churches above and before all else to take care that persons who are pious, learned, and excel in the knowledge of the Scriptures, who know how to divide the Word of God correctly, are installed as ministers and shepherds of the churches. No one doubts that the knowledge of the languages and sciences and continual practice in the exposition of the Scriptures (which are called meditations or prophecies) can contribute the most to this. And furthermore with a view to the future, whenever the churches are organized, in every possible way it will be important for the establishment and maintenance of unanimity in doctrine as well as in the regulation of ceremonies and discipline, as much as possible that frequent gatherings of neighboring churches be instituted so that every frequently occurring matter may be brought up for decision.

(2) Thus we think that the utmost must be done to institute first of all the institutions (scientific institutions) in which the three languages are taught, and in which a sound introduction and the exact practice of theology will especially flourish. Furthermore, work needs to be done to divide the distinct Dutch provinces up into defined and permanent classes, in order that each church may know with whom it has to deal and to consult with about all important matters that it thinks concern the general welfare.

(3) But at this point nothing can be determined about such matters before circumstances and experience dictate what places are most suitable for the respective matters. Therefore, we propose that, after the Lord has opened the door for the preaching of the Gospel in the Netherlands, all churches and all ministers of the churches will strive diligently to collect, as soon as possible, communal funds in order to call a provincial synod of the entire Netherlands. This legal synod will then be able to determine what in this matter and in all others ought to be observed concerning the joint structure of the churches and the maintaining of good order.[48]

Noteworthy is the fact that even in the face of severe persecution, and for their own safety forced to meet outside their own homeland, these ministers and elders laid hold of God's promises,

---

48 P. Biesterveld and H. H. Kuiper, *Ecclesiastical Manual, Including the Decisions of the Netherlands Synods and Other Significant Matters Relating to the Government of the Churches*, trans. Richard R. De Ridder (Grand Rapids, MI: Calvin Theological Seminary, 1982), 20–21.

convinced that the question was not "if" God would establish his church in the Lowlands, but "when."

One can sense the vibrancy of the confessions, yet so fresh, living in the mind of the believers in the Lowlands, "The Son of God...gathers, defends, and preserves for himself unto everlasting life, a chosen communion in the unity of the true faith."[49] "And this holy church is preserved or supported by God against the rage of the whole world; though she sometimes (for a while) appear very small, and, in the eyes of men, to be reduced to nothing."[50]

In that confidence these men gathered to lay the groundwork for a healthy, Reformed denomination in the Lowlands. In eight chapters they set down what they considered necessary concerning the assemblies and classes of such churches, the requirements of ministers, elders, and deacons, the importance of catechism instruction, regulations of the sacraments and marriage, as well as the requirement of faithfulness in the exercise of church discipline.

Three years later an official synod was constituted, held in Emden. Delegates from various consistories were sent to represent the Reformed "Churches Under the Cross" and in exile.[51] In Emden, convening in early October 1571, the first regulations for the order of the Reformed churches in the Lowlands were officially decided.

It is evident that in responding to the needs set forth by the gathering at Wezel three years before, the Synod of Emden was influenced by the decisions of the first national synod of the Reformed churches of France that had been held in Paris in 1559. Indirectly, the decisions of Emden were also influenced by John Calvin and the principles of ecclesiology that Calvin had restored

---

49 Heidelberg Catechism A 54, in Schaff, *Creeds of Christendom*, 3:324–25.
50 Belgic Confession 27, in ibid., 3:417.
51 Biesterveld and Kuiper, *Ecclesiastical Manual*, 13.

from holy scripture over several years of labor in Geneva and Strasbourg, as well as by John à Lasco and his work on church polity and liturgy while laboring among the Dutch Reformed refugees in London and in Emden, where he and his congregation had been forced to flee in 1553 when Mary Tudor became queen of England.

The first article adopted by the Synod of Emden established a foundational principle of Reformed church government over against the Roman Catholic system of a so-called divinely ordained hierarchy of clergy members and clearly followed the first article of the Synod of Paris: "No church shall have dominion over another church, no minister of the Word, or elder or deacon shall exercise dominion over another. Rather shall they be vigilant lest they should give cause to be suspected of desiring dominion."[52]

In addition, the Synod of Emden established the doctrinal unity of the churches by requiring the subscription of all ministers to "the confession of faith of the Netherlands churches," that is, the Belgic Confession of Faith, as well as the confession of the churches in France, for the sake of the French-speaking churches in the Lowlands. Recognizing these regional differences and differences in language, yet seeking unity in the essentials of the Reformed faith, the synod also decided that in the French-speaking congregations the Genevan Catechism would be used, while in the Dutch-speaking congregations the Heidelberg Catechism would be used.

The records of the early Reformed synods of the churches in the Lowlands indicate the careful attention given such matters as the confessional basis of the Reformed congregations in the

---

52 Duke, Lewis, and Pettegree, *Calvinism in Europe*, 158.

Lowlands, the calling of the offices of ministers, elders, and deacons, the form of Reformed church government, the exercise of Christian discipline, and the worship practices of the churches.

In the establishment of a Reformed church order, God provided for the continued development of the Reformed churches in the Lowlands. Decisions taken by these synods would establish a biblical form of church government with mutual oversight to see to the faithful maintenance of the truth and the faithful exercise of the offices and of Christian discipline within the Reformed congregations.

This is our heritage. It is part of the history of God's wonder work of grace in gathering and establishing his church in that region of the world where our churches find their roots.

God give us grace to be faithful as those upon whom his light has shined.